HUMAN COMPETENCE: IMPERATIVES

Books by Edward F. Berger, Ed.D. (a.k.a. C. Descry)
Free e-books available at MillennialBooks.com

Human Competence. 2019
Crow Canyon: Pioneering Education and Archaeology on the Southwestern Colorado Frontier. 1993. 2nd edition. 2009
The Early Years: Crow Canyon Education and Archaeological Research Center. 2016
Vital Lies: Analysis and Solutions to Critical Issues Facing Our Education System. 2012
Transcending: The Life of a Twentieth Century Man
Unscrewed: The Education of Annie
Cut Off: When Illusions Survive
The Spirit of the Sycamore
The Spirits in the Ruins
The Spirit of the Estuary
The Daughters of Onoto
The Brothers Shikoku
The Fallout Solution
Raven's Chance

HUMAN COMPETENCE: IMPERATIVES

EDUCATING FOR THEIR FUTURE

EDWARD F. BERGER
WITH DAN KENLEY

Contact Information:
Dr. Edward F. Berger
edwardfberger@gmail.com
www.edwardfberger.com

Dan Kenley
dkenley13@gmail.com

Podcasts with Dan Kenley and Ed Berger
insightsintoeducation.libsyn.com

Cover art by Karolina Stankevičiūtė

ISBN: 979-8-4045-2096-5

Give the pupils something to do,
not something to learn;
and the doing is of such a nature
as to demand thinking;
learning naturally results.

—John Dewey

Contents

Preface

Human Competence: Imperatives is a continuation of the virtual campfire learning environment that was used as a rallying point in the introductory book, *Human Competence* published in 2019.

The *Human Competence* series utilizes the model of a virtual environment wherein students are free to identify current and future issues and explore solutions to real problems they face at school and in everyday life. Through discussions of their individual and collective research, they demonstrate how problem-solving, collaborative learning, and instruction can take place. This approach to education works with children of all ages not only in virtual environments, but in communities around the globe.

Human Competence: Imperatives is not a slick how-to-do-it guide, but rather, it simulates what a 'real time' educational experience looks and feels like for students today. The antiquated structure of our education system has to change to prepare students for their future in a technology-rich world. The way schools work is changing so rapidly that everybody involved, students, parents, teachers, administrators, community leaders, and politicians, are confused. We all know the system is broken but differ widely in approaches of how to fix it. The false assumption that 'anyone can teach' underlies too many programs. Over a decade ago, Teach for America (TFA) began a trend of placing uncertified 'teachers' who have minimal training in classrooms with our children. The damage done to children is now forcing TFA to change direction.

Meanwhile, we are witnessing experienced professional educators who are trying to teach students to compete in a world dominated by machine-based data processors that are better at almost everything within quantitative fields. Students readily access these data-gathering and data-crunching 'intelligent' machines to expedite their search for information.

Within this world of artificial intelligence (AI), there are several levels of sophistication and development. Augmented AI is already a basic part of our daily activities. As we now apply it, it is a tool to enhance education and almost every human activity. It can be extremely useful, but it is not what is driving the future.

What we have learned is that the 'genius' level of AI is a Super Intelligence (SI). As these artificial intelligence algorithms become more complex, they are gaining the ability to mimic how the human brain works. SI is becoming an advanced intelligence in its own right. It is not confined by humans. SI has the capacity to go way beyond anything artificial intelligence controlled by man can do. That creates a problem for the homocentric thinkers who have long believed that man is in control and will remain in control of machine intelligence. As SI evolves, it has the potential to become a sentient entity; a new life form on our planet. This will create all kinds of ethical and moral debate about who controls SI.

Human Competence: Imperatives takes on the challenge of how to provide today's students with the skills and competencies to partner with SI for the betterment of all humankind not just massive corporations.

This quote from Neil deGrasse Tyson closely follows our philosophy of education:

> Good education is not what fills your head with facts but what stimulates your curiosity. You then learn for the rest of your life.

Some of the students involved around the campfire are real. Others are virtual composites of students we have had the pleasure of knowing through our combined 100+ years as educators. Let the learning begin.

Introduction

In 2018 and 2019, a diverse group of secondary school students, using avatars, worked together around a virtual campfire to identify the qualities *Homo sapiens* has, that machines, which collect and manage data, do not have. The focus of the 'campfire' virtual gatherings was to demonstrate how distance learning can be used effectively; how students can accelerate their learning, become self-directed and collaborate to solve problems. At the end of the project in 2019, their process was chronicled in the book *Human Competence*. Students not only identified human strengths that machine intelligence does not have, but they underscored the message that education must be redefined to focus on the world and skill sets of *their* future—not outmoded models and collections of standardized facts anchored in the past. With the burgeoning growth of Super Intelligence (SI), this shift has become imperative.

Education must teach and reflect human character, values, ethics, and critical thinking skills so humans can protect their rights, freedom, democracy, opportunities to contribute to society, and opportunities to achieve their full potential. Education must also be inclusive and versatile. Society must influence politics to fund public education to ensure an educated citizenry. Humans must learn to partner with and live in a society with artificial intelligence and an evolving super intelligence.

No one could have predicted that education programs all over the U.S. and the World would be forced to adjust to a pandemic and a reliance on virtual education. It has required us to take a long hard look at what we are doing in the name of education. The pandemic has exposed catastrophic divides which had been hidden or ignored in the existing system. As the entire system shifted and adapted, these divides and lack of access to opportunity and infrastructure due to poverty were once again laid bare. No one could have predicted a president who lied over thirty-thousand times with the conscious intent of undermining truth. Few expected an all-out attack on our fragile democracy. In less than two years since *Human Competence* was released, we were thrust into a future we didn't expect. We were not prepared.

With the onset of COVID-19, traditional formal education stopped. The school, the classroom, teachers, and parents were forced to abruptly adapt to stay-at-home education. Corporations rushed to profit from the virtual instruction opportunities which they touted could replace person-to-person instruction. Education testing companies that depended on obscene profits from mandatory standardized tests tried to require that their tests be given even though most students had lost almost a year of traditional instruction geared to standardized materials. Almost everybody made assumptions ranging from viewpoints that the students could never recover from the loss of classroom instruction, to the view that much of what was 'lost' was of little value to the students' future successes or failures. They pointed out that the one thing that would be hardest to recover was the time lost in face-to-face interactions, and that virtual Zoom rooms could not duplicate the dynamic learning environment of human interactions. Many families who thought virtual schools were the answer for the future of education, quickly realized its drawbacks as they worked first-hand with their children at home over the course of many months. Many children at or below the poverty line lacked devices to connect and participate and were left out. Dysfunctional families or those parents who had no way, time, or means to take on the role of educator were unable to help their children.

The pandemic brought changes that were never anticipated. It accelerated our evolution into a future we weren't prepared for. We were caught unaware and too many want to try to continue the way we were; to find the old 'normal'. They pretend that rebuilding the old system will ensure the future of mankind. Unfortunately, too much of humanity will be oblivious to what is happening and will be unaware until it is too late for them.

Solutions fall to those who do understand the urgency of the task to save humankind; to adjust our thinking and education systems so that they develop the strengths *sapiens* need to survive in the immediate future and beyond. The pandemic has made it abundantly clear that we humans do not have decades to gradually adapt to these changes. Change and adaptation are required now, within less than a decade, for our survival.

In the last few years, it has become evident that our species will share the planet with a Super Intelligence (SI) that was created by humans and is patterned after the neural capacities of the human brain. This artificial intelligence is far superior to all human brains combined, in its ability to gather and manage enormous sums of information (data).

A new paradigm for educational instruction in public schools is imperative in order for students and humanity to survive in a world with a super intelligence that surpasses human brain capacity.

Traditional standardized education programs that duplicate machine intelligence are, even at this early date, no longer needed. Humans cannot beat SI in the data-crunching game. An educational model that focuses on that endeavor is a waste of effort, resources, and a tragic squandering of human potential. When students are prepared to flourish in the technology-rich world of the future, they will learn to partner with SI and control its use as a tool to advance humanity. This possibility of hope for a positive evolution of our species, runs counter to those who would fall victim to the dystopian vision that the rise of SI will eventually wipe out our species.

HUMAN COMPETENCE: IMPERATIVES

Chapter 1

Building a Learning Team

Claire: "Doc, we have been trying to reach you. Remember me? Claire in Iowa? I feel this strong pull to get us all back together. I miss our campfire meetings. Do you know what happened to all of us? By the end of our last gathering, we all pretty much agreed that our process changed the way we learn and the way we think."

Dan: "Hey Claire! I hoped some of you guys were on. Hard to believe it has been two years since our last campfire. Remember me? I'm Dan from San Francisco. Claire you're right. I feel the same need to reunite our learning group. Seems like none of us can stop searching. Now that we know humanity is in such a critical state, I agree we need to stay in closer contact as we continue questioning and learning. To tell the truth, I think a lot of us are scared about the future."

Roberto: "I check this site pretty often to see if anyone else from our group wants to chat. I see that Claire is contacting Doc. This is great. I'm Roberto, in case you don't recognize me without my Avatar, lol ... Things here in Idaho are really difficult. Those who believe in science and facts are few and far between. I too, am afraid. The Hispanic community is more open to what I've learned, but the people here don't want anything from the 'damned Mexicans' except cheap labor. I feel so isolated. Claire, did Doc get back to you?"

Doc: "I'm here."

Roberto: "I've missed working with all of you. Claire told me she would try to get us all back together. Is there any chance we can do another research round like our other campfires? What did people think about the book?"

Doc: "The book we wrote is getting support from readers. I'm thinking about a Part Two; a second book in the series. Dan Kenley, a great educator, and I have been working together for several years. Dan, known as Mr. K, suggests we call it *Human Competence: Imperatives*. We will collaborate, gather research and write it together. I'm game to start another campfire class if you are. By the way, four new people contacted me and asked if I was going to hold another session. They have been bugging me to start one. Ron is originally from Arizona, but now lives in Europe. Susan is also from Arizona. Ken is from California and Dave is from Colorado. Dave spent three years in the Peace Corps. With your permission, I'll ask them to join us.

"Claire, have you heard from anyone else? I know Ben is back in Sicily and can't join us. George contacted me about a year ago and apologized. He represented himself as white of European origin. He wanted me to know that he is Black African. His avatar was white because, as a black male, he felt if he shared his true identity, he would be discounted. I told him, and I assume you all agree, that it makes no difference to us."

Claire: "Great! It sounds like you are willing to put up with us again. I'm excited! I've been in contact with Annie (Kansas City), Frank (New Orleans), Mary (AZ), and George (New York). I'll email them and see if they want to participate."

Mr. K: "Let's get everyone together one week from today and discuss what we want to accomplish in the next campfire."

Claire: "Okay! Sounds like a plan. I should be

able to contact everyone by then. Then we can meet at our virtual campfire around 7:00 pm AZ time, 10:00 pm Eastern, 8:00 Central and 6:00 pm Pacific. Ron is 9 hours ahead of us, so we have to factor his availability into our scheduling. We want to be sure to include him. Doc, will you forward the contact info to the four new people who want to join us?"

Doc: "Will do. As before, it will be a collaborative effort. We are both looking forward to working beside you as we keep refining the future foundations for education."

Chapter 2

The Challenges

Claire: "Okay! I think everyone is here. It feels good to be back together again! Where shall we begin? Annie? You messaged me that you have concerns that need addressing."

Annie: "Hey everybody! I'm Annie, remember? I still have a lot of fear about the future. I'm worried about the survivability of our species. I'm even questioning whether I want to bring children into this world. I'm wondering what will happen if we don't have the competencies necessary to stay ahead of the changes associated with the rise of a Super Intelligence (SI) that is like the prodigy level of artificial intelligence. I feel like someone, or something, is holding my head under water and I can't breathe. Where and when does this all end? Have we really created a form of 'intelligence' that will wipe out humanity? Are human beings really becoming irrelevant? I grew up with films like the *Matrix* and *Terminator*. I don't think I want to live in a future run by omnipresent and omnipotent machines. It is scary stuff and we need to figure something out sooner rather than later. What do you think, Frank?"

Frank: "Hey Annie. I'm glad we're back in touch again. You ain't the only one with a belly full of fear. Yours is a such a common point of view. The last years of myopic narcissistic thinking and GOP misdirection during the Trump presidency has unleashed a culture that lacks a moral compass and honors lying. It's unbelievable but sadly, it isn't entirely new! In the U.S. it tracks clear back to the Reagan administration. Remember the lie they forced on America with the publication of, 'A Nation At Risk'. It was one of the first major attacks designed to destroy public schools. The more I read about it, the more I couldn't believe the terrible damage it did to our schools. No wonder people believe lies over facts when they are not taught critical thinking.

"I think we all share the fear that it's too late to do what we must do to retake the system. Every article I get my hands on contains some dystopian vision. There is no hope for unskilled labor. Public schools are being replaced by schools run for profit, not for kids, and definitely not for the benefit of society. The family unit is breaking down and single-parent homes now outnumber two-parent households. Prisons for profit are everywhere and the public is stuck paying the managing corporations for the beds whether they are filled or not. It makes it easy to rationalize policies that fill cells with people who cannot defend themselves. Authoritarianism is dominating politics and the fundamental underpinnings of democracy are being undermined. Yearly military budgets exceed infrastructure repair costs. The courts are stacked and the Constitution is being ripped up. It is so discouraging."

Mary: "Not only that Frank, I've learned that the power of Artificial Intelligence (AI) has now been surpassed by a Super Intelligence (SI) which absolutely fills me with dread. I understand why Elon Musk longs to '. . . look at the future without sadness.' I was just reading an article in the magazine *Fast Company*, (March/April 2021) that exposes Big Tech's influence over AI and the 'near total control' of industry ethics. Big Tech money is determining which ethics apply and which don't. More and more in-house ethics advisors are coming forward to reveal that their recommendations were intentionally ignored by the corporate leadership. Safiya Nobel is a professor at UCLA, and the cofounder and codirector of the Center for Critical Internet Inquiry. She says, 'This is about an industry that is broadly predicated upon extraction and exploitation and does everything it can to obfuscate. . .'

"Hey team, if most of us believe that SI will be developed with algorithms that are compromised and biased by corporate greed, how can we believe what is being developed is even remotely in humanity's best interests?"

Annie: "I agree Mary. What you just said scares the hell out of me too. I think we all agreed that education needs to become human-centered. We need to evolve away from being driven by corporate control and profit. Ethics is a big part of that equation. We are no longer in the Industrial Revolution, but too many of our working assumptions still serve that outdated model."

George: "I have serious concerns about the military issue that so dominates what we think and can do. It is mostly an economic issue. But there is data that supports war and military spending and perpetuation. That is assuming that the most sophisticated and powerful machine intelligence is linked to other computers that draw from the same data and come to the same conclusions. So, what would super intelligence tell us? I think the data, depending on the search criteria of the algorithm, would show that war is a waste of human and physical resources;

it is not efficient. So, war has to end. If there are no longer threats, then defense is unnecessary. War is out of the question. Soldiers go home. War equipment is available for salvage. We celebrate! But has the super computer (SI) considered the many millions of people who have lost their jobs? I wonder if the computer can come up with creative ways to re-employ them?

"We can't assume that super computers can evaluate situations from emotional and personal viewpoints. The most likely computer decision would be to get rid of those who are no longer needed. All of us here can agree that is a terrible idea on purely moral and emotional grounds, but some flesh and blood people in power with the values of a Hitler or Trump, could look at the data and determine, based on overall efficiency factors, that we should kill off a large sector of our population. At some point a human with human values has to step in and push the stop button."

Annie: "I would say that an education system that is focused on compassion, mutual respect, creative solutions, etc. would produce programmers that would take the world down a different path. There are always going to be a few Dr. Strangeloves in the world, but the goal is to tip the balance in a new direction. What kind of human can step in and stop this computer-based version of morality? If we are right, we are designing an education system that will produce that kind of person. What do you think Mary?"

Mary: "What we researched in our last series of campfires is really important. Frank, remember the human qualities we identified that computers don't have? These values must be the driving forces of our schools for the future.

Dignity, spontaneity, imagination, intuition, unpredictability;

Risk-taking, reasoning, analytical thinking, originality, initiative;

Critical thinking, emotional intelligence, spiritualism;

Flexibility, spontaneous, visualization, spirituality;

Contemplating the unknown, cooperation, and problem-solving.

"We all felt these are the attributes that will allow us to partner with SI and use it as a positive force."

Ron: "I agree with Annie. I too am nervous about the future, so I looked for some source that isn't painting a dark future. I looked for someone in the know who isn't afraid of what is happening. I watched a short presentation on YouTube by Duncan Wardle (TEDXPCL iHuman) who said, 'the rise of artificial intelligence should not be daunting.'

"Duncan puts forward his thoughts on why AI is our friend and what core human qualities it will never surpass. I'm not going to filter his work through my limited understanding. That's why I urge you all to watch and keep Duncan's work in mind as we go forward. Duncan spent 30 years at Disney. He was head of Innovation, and he achieved some incredible feats. The YouTube video is only 3 ½ minutes long."

Claire: "I think we all need to look at the future of SI from both sides. I like that you didn't try to filter and instead directed us right to this source."

Ron: "I'm not trying to be negative and devoid of hope. I know our generation is not responsible for creating the horrors we have suffered under the populists like those that are springing up around the globe. But the history I have studied tells me that what happened recently was the culmination of many years of degeneration. We have lived through one of the most disgusting periods in American history. The leader of a country, our country, whom many people supported—still support—valued lying over fact-based information, and not little white lies, but lies told to destroy; to undermine our concepts of what is true.

"Our younger generations are the victims of this decadent period. How can we believe that SI will be developed by corporations that are operating for the common good, and not for power and greed—we can't! Many people create corporations with a sinister purpose in mind; to hide the evil they do behind corporate veils, to limit their liability, and to hide from accountability. At their best they are amoral. Sure, what we want to propose is probably right and good, but the nation we inherit is so damaged and so many people joined in its destruction that we may not count. What do you think, Ken?"

Ken: "I agree. The society we envision is driven by love, emotion, empathy, creativity, critical thought, and cooperative-collaborative behavior. But when we propose it, we'll get pushed right off the stage. Too many folks think those qualities are weaknesses or completely toothless. And at the same time the Supreme Court has ruled that corporations are people

—maybe even superior to people—even though they have no ethics and little accountability."

Ron: "Hey, I read the book *Human Competence* and I admire what you guys did. Frank, I was reading Jay Tuck last night and he makes a point that AI (artificial or aggregated intelligence) is already here and that we are oblivious to the future it is creating. He's not the only one warning us about AI. But let's be clear; although he and many others still use the term Artificial Intelligence (AI), he is talking about Super Intelligence (SI)."

Frank: "Ron, who the heck is Tuck?"

Dave: "Let me answer. When I was in the Peace Corps in Africa, I became familiar with him. He is an American journalist. He founded Airtime Dubai and he worked with German television. AI is not just an American invention; people all over the world are warning about it. He recently did a Ted Talk called *Artificial Intelligence: It Will Kill Us*. I agree with Annie and I'm afraid of the future. But think about this! SI is pure data. In an ideal world there could never be a rise of authoritarianism or the cults that emerge from a contaminated spring. It's pretty clear that Big Tech has other motives. SI will be used against us. That is a given."

George: "Okay. I don't know about the rest of you, but I think you will agree that all of our research, analysis, thinking, and assumptions about education for the future, in fact, the future of our species, leads to a dystopian viewpoint. I hate to be so negative, but the fact is we don't have a future if we continue as we are now. We (the collective WE) have overpopulated our planet. We have abused life in every form and killed, mutilated, or in many ways destroyed other humans and lifeforms. We have high murder rates, prisons full of people we believe should be removed from society, and chemicals that kill other forms of life we think endanger our food supplies. We're pretty far down the road and wiping out our species is the next stop."

Dave: "George, I fear what you say is true but I still have faith in our ability to make better choices. I have to. We know about plagues, warfare, climate change, overpopulation, forced migrations, and just about everything that those of our species have experienced, done, or are causing. No neutral court would find that we should continue as we are. But is this the end? Humanity has rallied in the past and emerged from devastating times. Will SI and other predictable and data-driven intelligences replace us or save us as we implode? Can we save ourselves? What is the answer? What happens now? What can we prepare children for? Mary, Claire, Susan, you are nodding approval. Is this what you believe?"

Susan: "What can we do? We just went through a period in the USA where almost half of the population turned against rational thought. They rejected facts and allowed themselves to be manipulated by what can only be described as malevolence. This turn from decency, honesty, and morality has occurred many times before. The most recent in the Western world was Hitler and his cronies who subverted a sophisticated society. We believed that America had been vaccinated against and was immune to this infection of evil and the manipulative playbook. But I watched GOP rallies on TV and saw the faces full of hate and fear screaming like rabid animals. These are not the faces of the poor and suffering, but the vicious attacks of basically well-off citizens. They were orchestrated by fear, hate, prejudice, racism, and appeals to their selfishness and contempt for others. My point is that our species can turn on itself and revert to reptilian emotions at any time.

"There are more than seven billion people on our planet and most do not have tech advantages like WiFi or a mobile phone. Even if a majority of Americans change our schools, and if improved education for the children's future takes place, it probably won't make a difference. We, as we are, cannot survive. Our species cannot continue as is. Ken, Native American people died by the millions and there are only remnants left. What do you think? Am I wrong?"

Annie: "Wait Ken, before you respond to Susan let me comment here. God would never let this happen. He would never end our species. We are his people and the *Bible* sets us aside from other creatures. Oh, I admit that prejudice of those with darker skin is taught as an explanation of what happened to the descendants of Cain after he slew Abel. Dark-skinned people were viewed as inferior—not just then, but for thousands of years. And I know that slaves were necessary when those in control did not want to do hard work. In fact, we would still own human slaves if we did not have machines, our modern-day energy slaves. We still have forms of human slavery in prisons, in our fields, and in low paying jobs. God has to know what man does to man . . . and the forests, oceans, animals, the insects and tiny things. We are wiping them out. God created all things, but according to us, other living things are not protected, only us. Why would he protect us? Because he loves us and created us in his own image. That is why I can't believe that our species will end. Why are you looking at me like that, Ken?"

Ken: "Annie, that is crazy and mixed-up. If a god is involved, then that god is waiting for us to evolve into a more mature and wiser state. Mankind, as we know us through our actions through time, has demonstrated that we can be cruel and waste almost everything we touch. We are making this planet unlivable for our kind and other life-forms. We have in our hearts love and beauty, kindness and concern for others—really fine and important qualities, but these disappear when liars and the greedy rule and call on others of our species to destroy rather than build; to hate rather than love.

"The U.S., considered one of the most advanced nations on this planet, just went through four years of hatred, fear, destruction, bigotry, lies, and violations of the rule of law. Christian values like not lying, not stealing, not committing adultery, not killing, nor giving false testimony . . . were cast aside by at least seventy million Americans who knew better, but let themselves be overcome by hate. There is undeniable proof of the weakness of our species."

Doc: "Okay Annie, everybody, hold on! Venting our angst feels good but is the glass half empty or half full? For all the negative, where is the positive? This climate of fear that is so pervasive now is a large part of what we have to fight against. Right now, we are playing a game Eric Bern named as, "Ain't It Awful." Yes, it may be awful. It may be threatening and debilitating and defeating. But dwelling there isn't the solution. Should we just curl up and die? Do we drag awful into the future with us? We have to find a way to skip over or use awful as motivation to do what needs to be done to change things. As Gandhi said, 'Be the change you wish to see in this world.'"

Ron: "That's what we're doing. Once we get consensus on our direction, we will work together to figure out what we can do. Doc, I see what you mean about setting parameters. First, we need to make sure everyone is in agreement about our direction. Then we can do the research, inform ourselves, share with each other, dialog, and finally address some of these things so we know what we need to do. Working together we can incorporate everyone's input. This is a necessary and respected part of the process. Claire, what gives? Why are you so quiet? Remember you introduced us to Duncan Wardle? Now I see that we have reached the same conclusion that he did. Ken?"

Ken: "I want to have a voice, but in the past, every time I was in a group a few people did all the work and dominated the discussions. We're just kidding ourselves if we think that won't happen here. It always happens. As a Native American, I was always the minority. I was forced to sit quietly and when I did speak up, no one wanted to hear or understand my concerns. I was told I just didn't get it, or that my experience didn't map. We learned early on that to survive in school and this society we need to act dumb and wear a mask. George, as an African American you suffer the same insults. The dominant culture teaches that we are inferior and . . . well, if this process is really inclusive, be prepared for input from us you may not want. We may experience things differently and have views that are not popular. George and I might disagree with your interpretations and we're exhausted from being quiet and rolling over."

Roberto: "Those experiences are not unique to Native Americans and African Americans. I'm native born from Idaho and I go by Bob, but actually I'm Roberto Santos Escobar. I'm brown and a Hispanic American and I have many of the same experiences. Why are you agreeing, Dan?"

Dan: "Agreeing? Roberto, I am of Asian descent. I'm Chinese-American. White supremacists want to beat me up or kill me. They think if they can hit me or kill me, the 'Chinese virus' as Trump calls it, will end. The history of our ostracism goes way back. They hate me because I come from another part of the planet."

Susan: "I agree, as a woman I'm often afraid to engage in this type of discussion because men and even other women try to shut me down. But you know what? In a virtual world we are judged by what we know, not how we look or where our ancestors came from. I had no idea George was an African American. He could have been Georgette, or bright purple for all I cared."

Mr. K: "Ken, George, Roberto, Annie, Ron, everyone, campfires are organized around issues where everybody's opinion is heard and respected . . . and participants are working collaboratively to identify and solve problems that are real in their world. These are the ground rules of the campfire. They are the social issues that prepare us for community, political, and company work where people have to collaborate together to solve problems. It goes a long way in defeating bigotry and prejudice. I think these social issues are what schools are really all about."

Ron: "Thanks, Mr. K. I never had a class in school

like that. Did anyone? No one? Annie, you attended Kansas City schools. Mid-America has some great teachers. And you never . . . ?"

Annie: "No. As I think back, we were not involved in that way. We never worked with each other to solve real problems. Not even like, don't put crayons in the pencil sharpener. From elementary school on we were not working together to solve problems."

Claire: "Okay everyone. We are just going to have to trust each other. If someone feels like they aren't being heard, we each have a personal responsibility to speak up and voice our concerns. All opinions matter. Now! Let's get to work. We need to focus on changes to education. Maybe even pre-kindergarten. It's about teaching collaboration and problem-solving at every grade level. Doc and Mr. K, does that sound good to you?"

Mr. K: "We agree, Claire. Will we, the collective WE, introduce this from kindergarten up or do we work down from the upper grades?"

George: "So Dan, Claire, everybody, I think we are saying that we need to establish guidelines that will go from the lower grades through life. If we start with the foundations of education, won't we discover what works for the end product?"

Mary: "No, not necessarily. I really disagree. I don't know much about early education, but we're all here now and we know something about what we're experiencing every day. It seems like we should start where we are and identify the programs necessary to get where we need to be. I agree with Dan. If we don't know where we're going . . ."

Ron: "But Mary, can't we do both? I mean we have to see the whole picture. We can look at parts, but we have to have the whole continuum in mind."

George: "That makes sense. Our regular classrooms use the same old approach . . . teachers teach and students listen. Tests keep track of our progress. Our schools operate in a top-down, coercive way. They mirror our society. We know that way of teaching, filling us up with facts, focuses on skills needed to prepare students for a world that is long past. Thanks to AI we now have instant access to information. Of course, there are lots of acceptable things we want to keep like the basics . . . the skills of reading, writing, arithmetic, the scientific method, the arts . . . and critical thinking. But the issue, as I see it, is *how* these subjects are taught, the method as well as the content. When we are thinking about our future, I think we need to focus not so much on what basic skills need to be taught, but more on a different structure that changes the way students are involved in the process."

Mary: "I found this lady's work in which she clearly explains the models we operate under. I think it might help us develop some common definitions. Let me share some of Dr. Catlin Tucker's thoughts.

"Like many educators she entered the teaching profession with certain assumptions. She believed the following to be a true description of the traditional model of what is happening in our schools.

The teacher is the expert;

Learning happens in classrooms;

Students move from class to class on a set schedule;

Classes are composed of students who are the same age;

All students in a class should complete the same assignments.

"She states that '. . . these assumptions serve to create stagnation in the face of change agents. For example, if teachers see their role in a classroom as "expert", they design teacher-centered lessons where they spend significant time at the front of the room—physical or virtual—talking and transferring information. As a result, students spend much of their time quietly listening and receiving information.

"She asks: 'When you hear the words "teacher" or "student," what images come to mind? What is that person doing? What are their primary roles and responsibilities? How do they interact with other members of the learning community?

"Once we have unearthed our mental models and consciously understand what drives our thinking and decision-making about teaching and learning, we need to think about what we want teaching and learning to look like. We must encourage educators to design and facilitate learning experiences that:

> Place students, not teachers, at the center of learning;
>
> Prioritize student agency and invite students to make key decisions;

> Encourage communication and collaboration among students;
>
> Remove barriers and meet individual students where they are at;
>
> Leverage technology strategically to transfer more control over the time, place, pace, and path of the learning experience to the students.

"Dr. Catlin Tucker points out '. . . that to make long-term change, we have to construct new mental models that support and reinforce these new approaches to teaching and learning. If leaders and teachers value communication and collaboration among students, the mental image that comes to mind when we think of a classroom will include chatter, noise, movement, and flexible seating arrangements. We cannot say we value social learning and become anxious or concerned if we enter a classroom where students are talking and making noise. Our mental models communicate that a scene playing out in a classroom is either positive or negative. If leaders and teachers identify student agency as a value or pillar of learning, what will that look like in action? What would you expect to see in classrooms?'

"I have pulled this information from Dr. Tucker's

work. I think that if educators can change and move the top-down system to one of collaboration focused on student needs and on problem solving—based on real problems that must be dealt with, we can move away from standardized education, fact jamming, and deal with SI and the future.

"I want to add that Dr. Tucker and Dr. Katie Novak just released a podcast with George Couros *The Innovative Mindset,* which I recommend everybody listen to. They have also collaborated on a book that just came out about Blended Learning and Universal Design Learning (UDL). I know Annie and Susan and others have also discovered Tucker and Novak."

Dave: "Can I add some information? Claire, George and I talked back and forth when we researched their work. This is not a negative criticism. Every educator and parent should know what they are professing. Their work is based on the use of Augmented AI. We don't know how it deals with the concept of Super Intelligence (SI) that we are trying to differentiate and understand."

Annie: "That is to the point Dave. There is a history of the use of Augmented AI which deals with the expansion of teaching and almost everything using Artificial Intelligence. But recently man created a Super

Intelligence (SI) based on the way our brains work. It is not artificial, but as real as humans are in perhaps every way. Ken, we interrupted you. What's your take?"

Ken: "I attended Bureau of Indian Education (BIE) schools. We can all come up with examples of what schools did to us, or for us, and what we need for the future we face. I strongly agree with Tucker. We have to define a new system of instruction that is based on cooperative experiences. These experiences need to be focused on solving our real-world problems, not just a punitive system that assumes what is taught is relevant to our needs, but is really an attempt to standardize us for the benefit of those with power."

Susan: "I think I agree with you Ken, if you mean we must talk about the real issues we are facing like dealing with SI, the future of a floundering democracy, and ways to overcome the stagnation that has inhibited change. The way you and most of us were taught had little relationship to our needs or the world we will have to function in. Most of us were so far removed from society—to keep us safe they say—that we don't know how to participate or how things work. Right Dave?"

Dave: "I'm wondering. Is it too late for our generation? There is a slim chance some of us can change, but most will not. There is little possibility that real change can take place until the systems change for kids entering school now. We must focus on defining what changes are needed at this time which will affect the future of our species. I think this is it. I mean what are we going to do, Susan?"

Susan: "What if it is too late for our generation? How can we reverse the conditioning of so many years of schooling. It is so ingrained in us, and even more so for older generations - I'm not sure we can even see it. We are actively aware now that there are other options. Some of us can change, but most will not. You are right, real change will involve changing the system for kids entering school now. What do you think we should do?"

Chapter 3

Why the Old Education System Won't Work for New Technologies

Dave: "I like this process, but I've been thinking, I don't have a clear understanding of what is meant by, 'the structure that must be evolved'. This seems to be the key to what must be done, but . . . well, just what are we talking about? This is new to me."

George: "Guys, I've been reading Michael Fullan. Last time we researched together I looked him up on Wikipedia. Fullan is the Global Leadership Director, New Pedagogies for Deep Learning, www.NPDL.global. Deep Learning, as described by NPDL, is mobilized by four elements that combine to form the new pedagogies. They are: Learning Partnerships, Learning Environments, Pedagogical Practices, and Leveraging Digital. Change is a big part of his work. He describes what creates our systems as 'Drivers' and rates our present educational system drivers in this way:

1. Academics Obsession (selfish)
2. Machine Intelligence (careless)
3. Austerity (ruthless)
4. Fragmentation (inertia).

"Selfish, careless, ruthless, and inertia, are not things that we want to preserve. In the future he sees these types of things as the drivers of our systems:

1. Wellbeing and Learning (essence)
2. Social Intelligence (limitless)
3. Equality Investments (dignity)
4. Systemness (wholeness).

"Essence, limitless, dignity, and wholeness. I think we can understand where he is pointing. Is that where we want to be? I'm going to read more of Fullan's work. I want to know more about deep learning."

Claire: "I hear you, George. Susan has also been reading Fullan. Doc mentioned top-down coercive systems. That's the standard way the military, corporations, political parties, schools, businesses, and many American families are organized. Someone at the top of the power structure makes decisions. Sometimes there are boards, like our school boards, that select the leader who in turn selects the next level of leaders who then put the program in place. They hire the labor which is contracted to do specific things that meet the leader's agenda."

Mr. K: "In education, teachers are thought to be expensive hired labor who do what they are told—contracted to do—because the model is coercive. Teachers rarely determine the subjects taught and what is taught. They cannot plan outside of the limitations put on them by the top-down leadership. These limitations are usually not thought of as limitations on learning or hindrances to change. They are things like bus schedules, bell schedules, eating times, length of school day, selection and approval of materials and text books, where classes will meet, involvement in the community, means of measurement like standardized tests, and many other control-related factors."

Claire: "I know this because I was on the student

council at my high school. We were told we could be effective, but everywhere we turned, whatever we tried to do that did not fit into the prescribed system . . . well, we were coerced and denied input."

Annie: "The same thing happened to me, Claire. The system wasn't designed to take input from students or even parents and teachers. Politicians and pressure groups narrowed the curriculum and forced schools to teach what they wanted taught, and more disturbing to me is that these pressure groups are still having too much say in what schools must teach. My sister in 3rd grade is introduced to concepts that she does not have the cognitive ability to understand but she can say the words and pass the tests. Pressure groups, not educators, have forced the teaching of stuff that is not age appropriate. When we tried to improve things or have a voice it was obvious that we were just passing through the system like products on a conveyer belt.

"Some teachers who were really great started programs or activities that the administration didn't understand and pressure groups didn't like, like requiring students to participate in community activities outside of the classroom. They hit a wall and the programs were short-lived. They ran counter to the school model that was authoritarian. This is what you will learn and you will succeed if you regurgitate it back exactly as we trained you to do. No thinking outside the box.

"That process kills teacher creativity and the flexibility necessary to know the student and bring education to her. It totally kills student creativity. One important issue we wanted to address was the number of kids in school who were so traumatized by toxic home environments that they could not learn. We tried to introduce research from the ACE, the Adverse Childhood Experiences group. We were told there was no way we could add that information because the curriculum was full and there was no room."

Ken: "Claire, are you and Annie talking about reasons why? Even if we demonstrate the need for a change, the power running downhill blocks it."

Mary: "Ken, I would love to go into teaching, but it is being changed in ways that hurt kids. Many of my friends would go into teaching too, if they could teach and not be forced to inculcate. I love that word by the way. It paints such a graphic picture."

Claire: "Ken, that's right. Even if we demonstrate better ways of doing things, we need to be aware that we are proposing change that will be against what has been practiced since the beginning of . . . well, probably time. If we change to a student-centered program which is designed to empower students who work together to solve problems, we threaten those who have power and intend to keep it."

Ken: "In other cultures, things were not necessarily that way. There are models that were not top-down coercive. Some cultures had 'temporary' leadership based upon experience. They did not have one overall Chief, as the Europeans demanded, but a council of grandmothers, of elders who mediated and listened. My ancestors had evolved government away from power-holders and focused on best practices.

"Many indigenous cultures had . . . or still have . . . this form of democracy. That is one of the reasons they are wiped out. Representative government is a threat. In many states representative democracy is still a threat. The conquest was of European, often barbaric practices vs. those who had different values. If you have an open mind, consider the position of women in America today. Even with the 14th Amendment, women are still fighting for rights that were not in question in parts of this land until the European cultures dominated. The government, the military, those who had power would not recognize or even listen to women. In fact, they denied our form of representation and appointed one man to speak for us. They called him the Indian Agent and appointed a Chief who was expected to do their top-down bidding."

Mary: "Are you sure Ken? I don't think any of us have encountered that form of leadership in our lives so far."

Ken: "No, only now in the last several decades has personal worth, regardless of race, religion, gender, and ideas of superiority present in the dominating culture, begun to catch up to what many of us indigenous folks have known. You take a step forward and slide back. Progress is very slow. It was only one hundred years ago that you Americans recognized that Native Americans were human. As the expression goes, 'Mighty white of you.'"

Dan: "Listen Ken, you and your people have a real grievance, but what does that have to do with Oh, I see. We all have a lot to learn about human worth and how to create programs that treat all people with equal respect. My schools taught many conflicting values that mirror the ethics of our society at this time."

Roberto: "Stop! I agree with all that has been said, but we are ignoring the roadblock in the way.

Let's accept reality. Our technology has already created an intelligence that can process unbelievable amounts of information that human brains cannot begin to process. In fact, as the machine(s) gather this data, they can self-correct and self-teach, but they still analyze data using a binary system of '1s' or '0s'. This is the reality of our present and the future we must prepare humans to survive in. Most of the foundation courses we teach in schools have no purpose when computers can do those things faster and more accurately than we can. I found this article by Steven Johnson written in April 2020 called, *New AI Improves Itself Through Darwinian-style Evolution*. It is about a Google Project named AutoML-Zero, an approach that suggests that the future of machine learning may be machine-created algorithms. Deep Learning is a fast-developing branch of human development which Michael Fullan writes about and shares. I'm going to find out more about that. I recently learned that SI can now write its own algorithms. Ron didn't you read the same article?"

Ron: "Roberto, does it matter what we do if all of our efforts are a spit in the ocean? Damn, if what you say is correct, we are already living in a future we aren't prepared for—and it gets more complicated and troubling every day. Do we all feel prepared? We have grown up with Artificial Intelligence—Augmented Intelligence. It seemed like a boon more than a harbinger of doom. It's true, SI has the potential to be a threat, but in our world of education, consider that it can only standardize data and judge students by how well they give back what is taught. Is that really any worse than what we have now? It is still full of bias like many standardized tests. The construct of the algorithm may have been determined because it is thought to be culturally correct; because it fits certain race, gender, and social status beliefs."

George: "Roberto . . . Bob, how did you learn about SI? It seems like there is a whole new language evolving. We need to learn the terms, the names of things to help us understand what we're facing. We are struggling to get a grasp of how SI works. I bet we can safely assume that most of the people on the planet have no clue as to what is happening. Guys, we definitely need to research and learn more. This seems to be the topic that could drive these campfire discussions for quite a while. What's up Claire?"

Claire: "It's late. We are out of time, but that doesn't mean we stop learning. We'll get back together on Wednesday next week. Use every resource tool you can think of. Continue to educate yourselves. Let's see if we can define some of these terms. We need to build our knowledge base and vocabulary. Work together or alone, but let's take a look."

Chapter 4

How Do We Proceed?

George: "Hi everybody! We're all on. I've got some questions. Doing my research, I came across a guy named Robin Windsor who wrote, *Prep for the Future with AI*. He said that AI, in fact all technology, is developing faster than education can keep up. I second that idea. As I was learning more about machine intelligence, I came across this concept of a blockchain. I just don't get it. It is supposed to be the most advanced form for managing AI. I found this on Google. 'What is blockchain? Blockchain technology is most simply defined as a decentralized, distributed ledger that records the provenance of a digital asset. Geez! Can anyone explain it to me?'

"I tried talking to folks around here but no one I talked with understood that 'simple' definition. I did find that some people thought blockchains were great investment opportunities. I looked up ledger and found: 'Ledger—hardware wallet—state of the art security for crypto assets.' I wanted to know what crypto assets were. 'Bitcoin, Ethereum, XRP, Monero, and more.' Great. Three people I talked to had heard of Bitcoin, but none of the other stuff. I decided that a bunch of clever guys who were isolated in corporate offices and removed from the real world invented a new language that was unintelligible to people like us."

Mr. K: "Thanks for sharing, George. Sorry you started with a hard insight. It sure reaffirms how complicated things are. Anybody else had similar problems?"

Claire: "Thanks George for sharing your frustration and coordinating the responses. But if this is any indication of the new age, how can a normal, non-techie human make it?"

Frank: "Hey Doc, I have some concerns about what George experienced. I ran into some of that too. It's pretty hard not to feel dumb, confused and overwhelmed. This is way beyond making cellphones and computers work for us."

Doc: "No Frank, we are not limited in our development or lost. Let me tell you about a professor

I once had who was touted to be one of the great scholars on the Middle Ages. We used his text book in Humanities class and it was almost impossible to read. His lectures were so full of jargon and references to other scholars that his teaching went over our heads. He was the perfect academician. He had learned to complicate things in ways that hid his inability to communicate and made him seem like a highly intelligent man, which I think he was by the way. He was just a terrible teacher. He was so intellectual that he couldn't communicate with others. There are those who mistake this weakness for great skill. I think that what your group ran into as you wanted clear answers to new and complex ideas, are these types of individuals who understand the technology, but can only explain it using terms that come from the most technical side of their profession. I think you guys are doing a great job trying to cut through the BS to get the information you need. Good question. Frank?"

Frank: "The biggest problem I had was sorting through sources. I would be looking for a good definition of AI, which now I think is really SI, and then I'd get sidetracked with issues like what SI would do to the workforce. It did seem to confirm what most of us believe, that AI will soon replace most repetitive tasks and as a result many workers. If a worker is on an assembly line bolting on a part, then a robot driven by a computer functioning with AI can and will replace that person. More, that robot can run all day and night, in the dark and in the cold. Even in professions like law, attorneys using powerful search algorithms can compile all of the case studies that pertain to the case they are working on, can run win or lose scenarios, develop and experiment with the data to find winning arguments, draw conclusions, and present a road map for their case. Who needs law clerks? For the time being, management, skilled workers and professionals, will be secure in their jobs, but in the very near future, many of these jobs can be done by AI-driven data crunchers.

"It seems pretty certain that in the not-so-distant future we'll be sharing the planet with another lifeform—a Super Intelligent entity that can write its own algorithms. This is one of humanity's creations that is, in many ways, superior.

"It was hard to find a list of jobs or professions that could not be done more efficiently, possibly even better, by SI. I guess it depends on what type of educated populous we want."

Frank: "Ron, what did you come up with?"

Ron: "I had this experience recently that I think

exemplifies some of what we are talking about. I just finished buying a car. I went through this whole lengthy process. First, I had to deal with the bank to make sure I had enough money or could finance the amount I had to borrow. Once I jumped through all of their hoops, I had to find a car I wanted and could afford. Then I researched things like models—I wanted a small economy car, maybe a hybrid. I found sites like 'Kelley Blue Book', and got an idea of what cars like I wanted were selling for. Then I started looking for a car I could buy. I found checklists which helped me—for example, condition of the oil on the dipstick and evidence of repairs to the body. Had the car ever been in a wreck? Was there an 'S' on the title. Did I like the color? Were the pedals worn and was there evidence that the mileage was accurate. Brakes? Tires? I went through the checklists and found the car I wanted to buy. Then I had to get a certified check for the seller. I had to meet her at the bank and get the title notarized. Then I had to go to the motor vehicle office and get plates and a new title. Then I had to contact my insurance company and get liability insurance, because after researching types of insurance I realized that I did not need comprehensive coverage. What a learning curve!

"When I got home, my dad asked me why I had gone through this process to get transportation when all I had to do was call a company like Uber, and order-up a car when I needed it. All the steps, the research and the frustration I went through were unnecessary. New systems are evolving rapidly. The use of SI and massive data collection could speed up or replace whole processes that we once thought necessary. That is gonna be one of the benefits of high-tech in our future. The world as we know it will be a memory."

Mary: "So Ron, are you saying that the way we are trying to get information is a waste of time?"

Ron: "A lot is, Mary. There may be a more efficient approach. In times past, a man needed to know how to put the harness on a horse before plowing a field. In times past, we had to go through a process like I went through to get transportation. Now transportation is conveniently available upon demand. They are already fine-tuning the prototypes for driverless vehicles."

Dan: "I agree. We know machines can use mathematical processes that a human mind, given a lifetime of study, can't master. As we rely on them more heavily though, we need to learn the 'language' of a world which has SI in it. We need to learn how to communicate with super computers and intelligences that crunch massive amounts of data and make decisions about the most economical ways to do things. I think we need to continue to brainstorm and prioritize the unique skills humans have that differ from machines."

Susan: "I believe humans are good at some things and machines are good at others. A program could be used to analyze the most efficient and productive planting of a home garden, but the tending of the plants and the soil, the reciprocity and delight that is generated, is a distinctly human pursuit. I think we can create an education system that not only assures our survival as a species, but lets us use the power of SI to move us into a healthier place where we can find balance, end war and human brutality, and create a species that has earned the right to expand into the universe."

Mary: "Susan, I'm glad to hear you say you believe we can partner with SI. This is not the end, but the beginning. Clearly the systems that have evolved during the last few centuries no longer apply. They are being turned on their heads and being replaced. I think we can identify specific areas to work on as a group, even acknowledging that much of our future is unknown to us. Let's get back on track and make it so."

Claire: "Frank, George, Ken, everyone—you are nodding like you agree."

Frank: "The only sure way of failing is if we don't try. We all made the commitment to this process of discovery. I've already learned a lot."

Dan: "The problem is how do we proceed? I'm still not even sure what SI means. I think we should continue to define it."

Claire: "I have been searching the web for other groups that are working on future impacts driven by a heavy reliance on SI and AI. I googled 'the future' and got to Amy Webb's *Future Today Institute*. Their list of concerns includes: robots taking our jobs, the Internet of machines, flatter organiz ations, 3D printing, nano-technology, mobile apps redefining service industries, the fight for control of the mobile payments system, reinventing entertainment, the fall and rise of social media, and newspapers ceasing to exist.

"The article refers to *ovations.com*, where I saw even more predictions. Data rights become an issue, the DIY economy continues to rise, a new education revolution, retraining the work force, older workers re-entering the work force, dealing with a society at retirement age, China moving up the value chain, rising incomes in South Asia and Africa, the great deleveraging, and taming the big data tsunami.

"It confirms what we have been saying. If even a small part of this comes to pass, we are going to need different skills to make it. They mention retooling education, but I still haven't found anything that details what these recommended changes in our education system would look like."

Roberto: "Wow, Claire I'm on the sites now. Lots of material, mostly about dealing with current problems. I went to *A New Education Revolution* and found it was about online learning. I'm sure the COVID-19 scares put that on the list. We are talking about a major education revolution that must take place if humanity is to not only flourish but survive. I hope others are also aware that the way we educate is critical to the future and all the issues mankind has to deal with. Annie, everyone, please help me go through the list and pull out issues that have real meaning to education reform. I think 'the Internet of machines' is relevant to our studies. Also, 'robots and computers talking to each other.' We've been talking about 're-skilling the work force', which is about education."

Susan: "Here's another one from my Google search we should add. 'Deep Learning'. Remember?

George tagged it earlier. It's an SI function that mimics the workings of the human brain in processing data for use in detecting objects, recognizing speech, translating languages, and making decisions. It says, 'AI is able to learn without human supervision, drawing from data that is both unstructured and unlabeled.' That definition could be our starting point, except Super Intelligence is far superior to Artificial (Aggregated) Intelligence:

> Deep learning is a subset of machine learning (all deep learning is machine learning, but not all machine learning is deep learning). Deep learning algorithms define an artificial neural network that is designed to learn the way the human brain learns. Deep learning models require large amounts of data that pass through multiple layers of calculations, applying weights and biases in each successive layer to continually adjust and improve the outcomes.
>
> Deep learning models are typically unsupervised or semi-supervised. Reinforcement learning models can also be deep learning models. Certain types of deep learning models—including

> convolutional neural networks (CNNs) and recurrent neural networks (RNNs)—are driving progress in areas such as computer vision, natural language processing (including speech recognition), and self-driving cars.

"Here is another explanation that I got from GrowthTribe on YouTube. It talks about the difference between artificial intelligence, machine learning, and deep learning. AI exists when a machine has cognitive capabilities such as problem-solving and learning for example' (we've been calling this ability SI). AI has reasoning, speech and vision. So we can say AI has three levels. NARROW—AI when a machine is better than us in a specific task. GENERAL—AI, when a machine is like us in any intellectual task. STRONG—AI, when a machine is better than us in many tasks.

"These are some of the additional notes I took while I watched the Growth Tribe video.

"Machine learning is when algorithms are trained to use past examples and data sets, to get information sorted by trained algorithms, to create new data sets, and to get or apply new combinations.

"Deep learning makes use of deep neural networks. Shallow neural nets use multiple inputs, combined functions, and a focused output. Deep neural nets have multiple inputs, multiple combinations of functions and associations, and a focused output. This deep learning is particularly useful in image recognition and it is being applied to education.

"Don't look at me that way. I'm just getting used to the vocabulary and trying to tie it into something I know. Our chance of understanding and applying the concepts will improve the more we work with them. I'm still working on our use of the term SI as this form of machine learning moves beyond artificial or aggregated intelligence."

Annie: "Susan, does this mean that a system that mimics the human brain is in itself a brain, a machine brain, a Super Intelligence (SI)? If so, can it do everything a human brain can do? Is there anything it can't do?"

Susan: "I think it does, Annie. Our brains work because certain traits are inherited. Can we call them our basic algorithms? Then our brains are filled with data collected by our five senses, right? If any or all of the senses are missing then our brain cannot collect the data necessary for complete cognitive thought or it amplifies the other senses to create a work-around. The data we collect can also be skewed by misinformation or peer pressure. Are machine brains subject to the same weaknesses?"

Dave: "Susan, how do you know all that?"

Susan: "I typed 'facts about the way the human brain works' into the Google search engine."

Dave: "So, SI can have the same weaknesses we do?"

Susan: "Probably not, because SI uses more data than it is possible for human brains to gather. It may even be able to evaluate its original algorithms and improve them. Although, the construct of the original algorithm will by its very nature include the creator's bias. Is SI a superior form of intelligence? Or does it have its strengths and weaknesses like every other entity including humans?"

Claire: "For those of you who are new to the group, in our last campfire series that was documented in *Human Competence*, we spent a lot of time identifying the human competencies that machines don't have; how humans are different than machines. This is a thumbnail of the human characteristics that schools need to emphasize that prepare students to create positive outcomes in a world filled with SI. It takes time to think about each one.

Dignity, spontaneity. imagination, intuition, unpredictability;

Risk-taking, reasoning, analytical thinking, originality, initiative;

Critical thinking, emotional intelligence, Spirituality;
Flexibility, visualization, contemplating the unknown.

Cooperation and problem-solving."

George: "Dave, Susan, everybody, I think we agree that we are talking about designing an education system that prepares us for a world where SI is a major part of almost everything. We want to be able to see it used for good purpose; to improve the ongoing balance and stability of our lives and the natural world.

"You are right, we're back to using those human competencies as a spring board to enhance and build the education system for the future.

"It is a given that SI will collect massive amounts

of data about us. What if it decides that it should be in charge? How many movies have we all seen with a dystopian view of the future? The evil programmers manipulate the algorithms for their own nefarious purposes leading to the obliteration of humankind. What about androids like *Star Trek's* Data? Will there be fail-safes built into the programming that can't be violated? We may think we are much more enlightened than our actions indicate."

Roberto: "I'd say it is debatable that we humans are a superior form of intelligence. Many other species on the planet would probably disagree. We may have qualities that, if developed make us superior, but there are also qualities that make us dangerous and quite inferior. SI may decide in the very near future that humanity is too destructive; the species can't be salvaged; that the dark side of the human psyche overwhelms the good. Whew! That is a bleak thought. What do you think, Dave?"

Dave: "Let's look at it this way. We must design SI so that it can be . . . 'vaccinated' against programs designed by people who have evil or unethical intent. We can use SI for good, and let it sort out the bad. We have to believe that there will be enough ethical people in the world to oppose the negative forces that drive so many humans. Otherwise, what's the point of having these discussions? We're doomed, so we might as well forget it."

Ken: "I agree we should be working on that premise. I suggest we keep searching for those human qualities that can't be replicated by machine intelligence and figure out how to evolve instruction so that it enhances human qualities that are positive and good for all. Of course, the idea of positive and good for all is a bit subjective too, don't you think?"

Mr. K: "Let's try this. Who is the person you revere most? One living American who embodies the attributes we are talking about. The person that puts words into actions. A person that is working to create a world filled with compassion, justice, balance, mutual respect, and diversity. We do have models and heroes, don't we?"

Annie: "I have one. He was president. His life has been an example of the better aspects of humanity. Jimmy Carter."

Dan: "I agree, he is my choice too, Annie. Anyone else pick Carter or . . . someone else? If you didn't pick Carter speak up."

Claire: "Well, twelve agree. We have our model. Why did we all pick him?"

Ken: "His wisdom makes our work easier. I think we all saw his comments in *Guideposts*, which were on Facebook recently. When he was asked, 'What are the things that you can't see that are important? He gave the following answer:

Justice
Truth
Humility
Service
Compassion
Love

"You can't see any of those, but they're the guiding lights of a life."

Susan: "My friend Vila from Colorado shared this and I think a large number of people think this way. 'The strengths humans have don't come from the Id or even the Ego. It is not about 'me', it is about 'we.' It is part of the spiritual nature of people from all over the world. It transcends religious institutions and is a universal human quality."

Roberto: "Susan, I agree. These are qualities

that reside in all human beings. Too many people have not been taught to rely on them to guide their actions. Even people we think of as vile and evil must have some connection with these human qualities—even people who draw mostly on their baser animal natures; their reptilian minds. Somehow they have grown up disconnected from human dignity."

George: "Susan, we should add dignity to our list. I found this from Dan Rather, another person I respect. It is almost like a meditation or a chant. He said:

I hope
I mourn
I pray
I love
I listen
I resolve
I share
I waiver"

Ken: "These are human qualities similar to what my grandfather taught me; passed on from what his grandfather taught him."

Susan: "Ken, a friend of mine who loves nature

and the ancestral ways of indigenous people recommended this book to me. I really like it. It gives such a different perspective. I recommend that everyone read it. Native American author and botanist Robin Wall Kimmerer wrote *Braiding Sweetgrass: Indigenous Wisdom, Scientific Knowledge, and the Teachings of Plants*. It came out in 2013. She identifies key elements of detecting loving behavior, which is obviously human and not tech knowledgeable. She describes loving behaviors she learned from her Elders:

Nurturing health and well-being

Protection from harm

Encouraging individual growth and
Development

Desire to be together

Generous sharing of resources
Working together for a common goal

Celebration of shared values

Interdependence sacrifice by one for the other

Creation of beauty"

Ron: "Ken, if SI is able to provide us instantaneous access to facts and calculations, maybe now our schools can finally focus on the wisdom we have failed to teach. These and the points Carter and others have made could drive our education system. Michael Fullan points this out—we were given a message that is wrong. We are told that our scores on the SAT and ACT determine our future and that our scores on standardized tests are indicators of our worth. Those testing companies are still making disgusting amounts of money by insinuating that they hold the keys to human success. I found this quote from Chris Hedges that rang true with my understanding.

"'We've bought into the idea that education is about training and "success" is defined monetarily rather than learning to think critically and challenge students. We should not forget that the true purpose of education is to make minds, not careers. A culture that does not grasp the vital interplay between morality and power, which mistakes management techniques for wisdom, which fails to understand that the measure of a civilization is its compassion, not its speed or ability to consume, condemns itself to death.'"

Frank: "I really like the sound of that, Ron. Unfortunately, I grew up without those values, didn't you? As I was growing up, I believed our leaders and teachers were right and I conformed to their messages. But Ron, have you ever heard anyone say that you exemplify the finest qualities of humanity because you had a high SAT score? I'm sure you had people tell you that you are a failure if you had low scores."

Ron: "I agree Ken. What some Indigenous people know and what a very few teachers and parents know, is that institutions like schools should be teaching, above everything else, how to be effective human beings. We are not computers and robot machines. We are each of us unique, and like the natural world we live in we grow, bud, and blossom at different times together. Sure, it is a goal to learn to read by third grade, but some take longer to mature, some have rooted in richer soil, some have more immediate access to nutrients, more sunlight, less shade. . . . We are not machines. We are not widgets. We are biological beings. We have qualities that we assume machine intelligence cannot duplicate. Schools must cultivate those qualities and come up with a human-centered means of evaluation to chart growth. That and an excellent crap detector to sort fact from fiction."

Frank: "Ron, I agree our schools have been designed to inculcate skills and qualities that now computers and SI can duplicate and do much better. Our model will change that emphasis. The culture will shift and different priorities will emerge. My hope is that SI will be encoded by people with a different set of priorities and world view."

Claire: "We're making progress. For every hour we spend at the campfire, we are spending uncounted hours researching and learning. We have information at our fingertips. And we are each, in our own ways, digging and sharing what we have learned."

Mary: "Thanks Claire. Good observation. We all need time to dig. Let's break here and get together next week at this same time."

Chapter 5

Changing Our World View

Claire: "We are all present and the campfire is burning. Hey Ken. I see your chat message that says you have something to share with the group."

Ken: "Claire, everyone, while I'm not directly from the Siksika Confederacy—what you call the Blackfoot, the First Nation people of Canada and Montana—I do have relatives that are Blackfoot. In the thirties and forties, a man, named Abraham Maslow visited the Confederacy. He was developing a hierarchy of human needs beginning with the base physical needs of the body and ending up with self-actualization. He based the form of his model on a closed pyramid.

"Blackfoot people think in terms of a tipi that is open to the sky at the top. We believe that knowledge of the self is oneness with the whole of the universe.

We put being present and open to the life force of the universe as the foundation for human development. Community Actualization comes next. Then Cultural Perpetuity. Above that is the expansive concept of time and multiple dimensions of reality.

"He did not understand that we think in terms of tipis which are triangular but open at the top. Where his pyramid closes with the dominion of man, ours continues to expand. This maintains an active ongoing connection to the natural world. No species, including human beings, dominates.

"It took me many years to sort out these very different world views. I had to understand Maslow-type thinking and his definitions of mankind vs. the things I was taught by our Elders. I think it is the First Nation view of connection and respect for all things that we find reflected in the competencies that we are defining as critical for our future survival. It is what differentiates us from machines and is uniquely human."

Dave: "Ken, check out this First Nation perspective presented by Dr. Cindy Blackstock at the 2014 conference of the National Indian Child Welfare Association. I'm paraphrasing her comments. If Maslow had included the First People's perspective when he presented his hierarchy of needs in 1942, he would have been laughed off the stage. If he had presented the 'expansive concept' it would have been discounted as superstitious pagan blasphemy. The conquering European culture discounted the advancements of those they were trying to destroy. Ken, you say it fits with the way you were taught at home?"

Ken: "In my way of thinking the Europeans brought their ignorance and their God to the new world. They had hundreds of years to develop wrong thinking and beliefs that supported conquest and infallibility."

Mr. K: "Okay, Dan, Ken, Ron, Mary, Dave, Frank, Susan, George, Annie, Roberto, Claire, Susan, Mary—everyone. What you are saying is that some other cultures had or have beliefs that are applicable today; that offer a framework for living that is very different than what we embrace. If we shifted our perspective, our priorities, to include an approach that is more inclusive, focused on reciprocity and mutual respect, it might help us define a critical part of the foundational goals of our school of the future.

"Most of us have been raised to believe, like Maslow did, that our concept of the 19th century man is the ultimate form of humanity. But Ken, you just pointed out that other cultures defined man as evolving, growing, and changing; one species among many; no more or less important. Most of us think our species has evolved far beyond any others on the planet. It is a form of narcissism, disrespect and arrogance. What we are becoming aware of is that most of our institutions, based on that model, do not fit in the future. Our egocentric view of the world is leading to our extinction. I think we're right, but can you imagine trying to convince people that what worked to get us this far will not work anymore?"

Dave: "This sounds a lot like the Peace Corps model. I don't think we can convince people. All we can do is identify what must change, begin to incorporate world views based on humility and mutual respect, give up the notion that everyone and everything is a commodity to be owned, and describe an education system that will allow humans to partner with a new player in human evolution: SI and machine intelligence.

"By partner, I mean we must fit into this new phenomenon that is real and is changing almost everything—like work and education, access to information, and the definition of what it is to be human in balance with each other and the natural world. Claire, you introduced us to Duncan Wardle. In the YouTube video he interlaced his fingers to demonstrate the partnership with SI."

Claire: "How did all this happen so fast? This might begin to make sense to us as we research and share ideas, but most of the people on Earth have no clue, or are unwilling to give up their current world view that everything is ours for the taking. How . . . ?"

Dan: "Well Claire, some people choose to ignore the seeds of our destruction. They have another drink, take another toke, decide to live in some isolated place, don't have kids, and don't worry about saving money or social security. They just want to pull the blankets up over their heads and wither away as all of the support systems no longer function. They can all just die out and leave the world to creations that will continue on without them and potentially continue to wreak havoc."

Frank: "Whoa, whoa, whoa! Hold on a minute! Let's throw another log on the fire. Enough of this talk. Yes, there is an awful side, but I thought we agreed that what we are doing is developing a way to adapt to the changes that are already well underway for the improvement of humanity and all living things. We can't be the only ones on this course. Have faith that what we learn can be shared and that it will make a difference. Ken has pointed out that we have moved beyond Maslow and into the evolution of human kind."

Chapter 6

Challenging Old Assumptions

Claire: "Annie, what are we doing? Have we grasped enough of the basic concepts? Can we start to figure out how we might implement some of our ideas?"

Annie: "Susan, you guys joined us for this Imperatives stage . . . are you comfortable if we start to flesh out our ideas into concrete recommendations? Speaking for myself, I'm ready. I know there are some concepts we only grasp in cursory ways, but I'm sure we will continue to learn more as we work on solutions. Frank, I see you are waving your hand. What's up?"

Frank: "My concern is that we're preparing to come up with changes that we only assume will be needed. I guess I'm way behind you all. I think that before I'm ready to implement new views, I need to know more about what we take for granted and set aside the things that have no bearing on the future. I mean . . . take the concept of work. Generally, we believe that if you don't work, you don't eat. How often have we heard that? I guess that came from a time when everyone had to pitch in and do their share. But gradually, we humans developed systems where many could choose not to produce anything; to live off the labor of others. They developed systems that allowed the few to tithe or tax or invest so they could profit from workers and become the dominant class. Some folks could 'send out a dollar to bring in a friend,' as my Pa would say. Some actually created jobs by investing in companies that were hiring workers.

"Our political leaders and most religious leaders are paid by those who labor and create wealth. Now, with SI and robotics replacing workers to do what is referred to as 'redundant work', a major part of the system of production by human hands is disappearing. Workers are becoming 'redundant'. I saw a story in the news about a 'farmer' who can farm 10,000 acres. He uses computer modeling and AI to schedule, plant, fertilize, harvest, and control equipment in the field. Like a self-driving car, the farmer's work is now managing technology."

Mary: "Frank, I agree. But we are not talking about making changes to the developing systems like

AI and machine intelligence. We have to figure out how to evolve human capacities to survive and lead in a future which is already defining itself. Different types of jobs will emerge. Our concept of work in the future will revolve around being more creative respectful human beings while machines handle the work in the field. As we rely more on AI augmentation, we will be freed up to focus on cooperative problem-solving, building community, balancing resources, protecting natural systems, and ensuring quality of life for all. These are the underpinnings of a different world view that no longer embraces the notion that everything is a commodity. The industrial model that has driven our education system for so long is no longer relevant. And neither are the standards that are inculcated in our schools. That is the opposite of what humans need. It's like Fullan says that we need new drivers."

Ron: "Frank, it's not that SI makes humans irrelevant. It is that we have to accept that it is worthwhile and important, a valued goal to spend our time on other types of activities. We have to learn how to reframe our definitions of self-worth and success. What will we do with ourselves once we have all this time? Do we need a work identity to exist and feel valued? What do you think, George?"

George: "So, ironically, in this evolving world of ours where machines do the heavy lifting, we are going to have to be more focused on collaborating with each other. With all this info readily available, we can draw from a wider range of sources and have time to experience and deep-dive into different disciplines. We are learning that the world is more interconnected than we think. Life is not divided into separate subjects. It is a complex interwoven whole.

"While you were talking, I've been sitting here on my porch thinking about my experiences in school. I can't remember much about elementary school, except that on the playground we were in gangs with the bigger kids beating up on the littler kids. The white kids were always beating up on my black friends and me. In middle school, I remember we had classes in different rooms. We went to Mr. Smyth's room for Science and Ms. Collin's room for English. Now that I think back, the disciplines were separated. It seems so foolish to me now. They should have been teaching us how to weave all the subjects together; to merge English, math, social science and music.

"I'm sure my teachers were never expected to compare notes or work together to coordinate what they presented and when. Now that I'm out of school, that seems strange . . . I mean that was a standard practice in grades 6 through12. I wish I could remember if elementary school was multi-disciplinary. What I do remember is sitting looking out the window or at my desktop wondering why the girls were so full of energy and going along with really dumb stuff the teacher did. I got by because being a black youngster, the teachers had no expectations for my success."

Dan: "George, we moved around a lot. Every school I was in was exactly like you describe. The word 'interdisciplinary' was not in the education vocabulary in those days. Claire, are you nodding in agreement?"

Claire: "I guess I fit the model of the girls you were describing except it didn't seem dumb to me. I loved elementary school. It wasn't like you describe. It was the boys who were constantly doing dumb stuff like fighting, shooting spit wads, or teasing us. That's what made it hard to focus and learn. The teachers I had in grades 1 through 6 had to teach for us girls, because most of the boys were too immature to sit still. Middle school was a little different, and more of the boys had learned to cooperate. But . . . even in high school where we had several male coaches who taught classes, the boys, unless they were athletes or geeks, were a problem."

Susan: "Gosh Claire. It's been that way since our

schools were designed hundreds of years ago. Boys get in trouble and girls adapt. I think girls are better suited to that type of environment and style of learning. They mature at a different rate than boys. Some women teachers have very little sympathy for boy energy. But in defense of boys, I went to an all-girls elementary school. Every year there were several girls in each class who were considered disruptive—you know, high energy, questioning authority, joking around and acting out all the time. Our teachers were nuns, and wham, did they put those girls in their place—which according to some had not been dug yet.

"My take is that it is the system that is broken, not the kids. We need to look at an approach that works for most kids and brings the best out of them; boys, girls, minorities and those with different maturation levels. We need to start thinking about cooperative behavior, interdisciplinary approaches and integrated thinking. We need to teach all human beings from the time they are little how to work together, to embrace differences as a strength, and to focus on problem-solving."

Mary: "Claire, if working together in groups became the norm, with ground rules based on mutual respect, that would probably go a long way toward ending racial and gender discrimination. I mean, if groups of kids worked together to solve real problems that were important to them, if they were the engine and the teacher a gentle rudder that nudged them along the path to acquiring skills the kids need to master, while helping all kids to participate fully . . . school and life in general would be a whole different experience for all of us."

George: "Sure Mary. In an ideal world maybe. But how would we change a system like ours which has been in place for so long, to encourage collaboration instead of compliance and often competition? I think we need a dose of reality here. I was in classes with white kids. There were girls whose parents made it known they wanted no contact with a person of color. Even some teachers and the principal made sure we avoided contact.

"The amount of white privilege built into all our systems is unbelievable. If you're white you don't even see it. Ask a person of color what it's like to raise kids in this society. They have to teach their children a whole different set of responses to situations just to keep them safe.

"I was separated from white girls because they thought I would act inappropriately and force myself on them. I had to hide the real me behind a mask . . . all the kids from minority groups had to. All through school, I was warned not to look directly at white girls or talk to them. White guys protected the girls, and even in sports, they made sure I didn't make friends with white girls. I always had to be on my guard; careful not to get careless and find myself dangerously trapped. Imagine what those white parents would do if the school emphasized multi-racial work groups where everyone participated freely."

Ken: "George, you lived in the East, not the South. White supremacists where I grew up absolutely will not allow racial interactions in classes. If we proposed children working together, they would get violent in their attempts to put a stop to it."

Claire: "George, I am beginning to see that it is possible that our species has an ingrained fear of those whose color is different. I have been reading that we are all genetically 99.9% the same; that color differences are related to latitude, not inferiority or God's wrath. Most religions teach thinly veiled hatred of the 'other.' They may not admit it, but the oldest religions like Hinduism, and more modern religions like Mormonism, once taught that God is punishing people of color. I have learned that this is world-wide, and not just an American problem.

"I bet data is inherently color blind; does not

support racial bigotry or color intolerance . . . unless they specifically wrote an algorithm to detect it. We have to evolve the systems beyond hate and fear. Fear-filled people will petrify, they will not adapt . . . and adaptation is one attribute we will definitely need to cultivate to embrace the changes coming in our future. But you know what? SI, unless we contaminate it with our bigotry and sickness, does not care if we are male or female; white, black, brown or yellow. That is a plus."

Roberto: "It is awful . . . we have to be taught that inclusion is a better state of being than exclusion. Our world is getting more and more entwined. There is no avoiding the need to come together across cultures to stop this destruction of others and to meet future challenges. I agree with you George, dominant white narratives are so embedded in our culture that half the time I don't even realize how biased I am."

Susan: "Roberto, ours is not a totally prejudiced system, but it wastes people's true potential for sure. Here is my concern—at least at this moment. There is a lot of talk right now about reforming public education, and about using standardized tests to compare kids and schools across the country. How is that possible when the culture of neighborhoods and the cultures in various parts of the country are so different? We were just talking earlier about how we had such different childhood experiences based on our family backgrounds and where we lived. How can you measure individual progress in a situation like that? A lot of people calling for reform these days think the answer is using standardized tests to evaluate schools and teachers. How can that even apply when we are all so different? They think the solution is to make the system standardized, streamlined and cost effective through the use of technology. They want to take the human element out of education. We all know standardized tests with a one-size-fits-all mentality are not the answer. This is why. I read this quote from the late Karen Lewis, Chicago Teachers Union President:

> What many people do not know, is the use of standardized tests has its origins in the Eugenics movement. We have to be clear about the original purpose of standardized tests. In a society fascinated by statistics, we are often compelled to reduce everything to a single number. Those of us who work with children know that there are so many characteristics that cannot be quantified. Ask yourself whether you want to be part of a legacy born of the unholy

> alliance between the concept of "natural inequality" and the drudgery that has been imposed on many of our classrooms.

"I had never heard of Eugenics, so I looked it up on Wikipedia:

> Eugenics—Some common early 20th century eugenics methods involved identifying and classifying individuals and their families, including the poor, mentally ill, blind, deaf, developmentally disabled, promiscuous women, homosexuals, and racial groups (such as the Slavs, Roma, and Jews in Nazi Germany) as "degenerate" or "unfit".

"According to Wikipedia, the term eugenics was coined in 1883 by British explorer and natural scientist Francis Galton, who, influenced by Charles Darwin's theory of natural selection, advocated a system that would allow the more suitable races or strains of blood a better chance of prevailing speedily over the less suitable. Too often people confuse evolution with eugenics. I've learned that they are complete opposites. Phrenology was another odd practice that emerged at that time. People believed the bumps on someone's head could be read to determine if he/she was intelligent."

Dave: "Wait just a minute. You said that the system was streamlined by those who thought they could manage by data. You mean by testing, right? Not just testing where teachers check to make sure students learned what they taught, but standardized tests designed to make all students conform to predetermined outcomes. It doesn't seem like these tests measure any of the competencies we are identifying as critical like personal growth, cooperation and problem-solving. Like good citizenship. There is so much that we learn in school that cannot be measured by standardized tests. Tests like the SAT and the ACT and dozens of other measurement products add no value to human development. They are super biased and certainly aren't an accurate reflection of what the student has learned that will benefit him or her going forward. We've talked about this Ron, what do you think?"

Ron: "Remember the information included in *Human Competence*? The information from Yong Zhao that Diane Ravitch shared? Ravitch said, 'Pay attention to whatever Yong Zhao writes. He is among the very top tier of educational thinkers in the world. I always learn when I read his work.'

"Zhao said that China and other powerful countries did not have industrial revolutions because their government and customs required that all Chinese, to succeed, had to score well on standardized tests. That froze progress and thinking to conform with established norms that were inflexible. Zhao, is a brilliant thinker and educator. He recently pointed out that:

> Governments may decide to launch standardized assessments to track students' learning losses. It is possible that educational policy makers may be so interested in learning the extent of loss experienced by students that they will use standardized testing to assess all students. The desire to know the overall extent of loss and what achievement gaps may exist between different groups of students is completely understandable, but standardized testing can be the worst way to collect such data for two major reasons.
>
> First, any standardized testing given to all students will have a typically limited scope, with a focus on math and reading. In other words, what will be measured is not the entirety of students' learning

> but a small piece of their overall education. Even assuming that the assessments are highly accurate (which they are not), they would miss other equally and perhaps more important aspects of learning, such as confidence, self-determination, creativity, entrepreneurial thinking and other subjects."

Ken: "Exactly! I think we've all experienced this same limited thinking, or at the least the results of it. Is this our future? I don't think so. Does data analysis determine the future of humanity? Can the essence of our human experience and our thinking, living, experiencing human brains be fully quantified by a bunch of standardized tests? I don't think so. I agree with Zhao, if we only collect this type of data, and use it to sort out those who don't perform in the higher percentages, we will carve away many of the most creative members of our future society. We significantly undermine our hope to develop a creative class that can adapt to a rapidly changing world driven by SI. I think our species really would go extinct if we use data to justify a pass-or-fail system that eliminates even our most enlightened. What do you think Susan?"

Susan: "Fortunately, people are starting to understand the problems associated with these tests. When I started applying to universities this past winter, many of my first choices were not interested in SAT scores any more. They wanted portfolios. Top universities are seeing that a high score on an SAT is not a good indicator of success in school or in life. I wonder if the people at the top of the education ladder have written why the SAT, for example, is not a good measure of human learning and development? I'm going to find out."

George: "Let's take a break and regroup next week. We have a lot to think about."

Chapter 7

Not So Subtle Messages

Claire: "We're all on? It's like our bus driver used to say, 'If you are not here speak-up because we're leaving.' We are all accounted for including Doc and Mr. K. So, Susan, what did you learn about the SAT?"

Susan: "I read fifteen sources about the cancellation of SAT and ACT tests. Number one reason was that, in essence, the tests were skewed and there was little connection between university success or success in life. Kids with the lowest scores acceptable to universities often did better than kids with high scores. The second reason given was that because of the COVID-19 virus, the test results for 2020 were lacking. Not one article mentioned that the data collected did not indicate mastery of human qualities and human strengths. PBS NewsHour said, 'They have lost their luster as a common yardstick,' and that 'Universities already look at more than test scores'. I am thinking that in the past, where all their experience and knowledge lies, they were not trained to understand things like the nature of data-driven conclusions. I'm sure there are university professors and great thinkers who understand the future that is already on us, but they don't seem to be able to communicate this danger to their peers."

Frank: "And you think we can? Susan, how could we be aware when great minds who are proven thinkers and scholars, cannot?"

Susan: "We became aware. It started with the class researching those human qualities that separated us from AI-driven machines. The book *Human Competence* documented our journey as we broke through into this reality. I was ready for this challenge. Sometimes a breakthrough, even a small crack in what we assume is truth, lets through enough light so that others accept it as something they have always known. If we can open that crack to let the light out, the battle may be won or at least defined. Doc, what can you add to this?"

Doc: "Years ago, I worked with a great science teacher, Mr. Losasso, and he explained that very few scientific advancements were made without ruffling feathers. The religious leaders killed people—tortured and burned people to death—because the ideas presented threatened their world view. Of course, they did this for God so it was okay. Other ideas that emerged from observation of nature and astronomy were rejected because a majority of the people in control believed these observations threatened their power or because they upended the status quo. Ego got ahead of the scientific process and pursuit of truth. So here we are proposing that humans, regardless of color, race, gender, or previous condition of abuse should work together to solve problems. In these divided times that is threatening. The idea will be rejected by a large percentage of people, but that does not mean that we are mistaken."

Dan: "I think most of us agree, Doc. The white supremacist will believe we are contaminating the gene pool by any kind of contact. Anything that displaces their privileged, dominant, position. They will fight to keep their daughters pure. They will quote the *Bible* and say they represent God's will. But really, it's all about their power, control, self-interest, fear-mongering and greed. White supremacy is being talked about a bit more openly these days in the media though. That is encouraging."

Ron: "I think that the more teachers encourage students from diverse backgrounds to work together, the more likely these barriers will begin to break down. As teachers get students working together using collaborative instead of competitive models, these kids will move up through the grades and become unbiased citizens who work together to solve community problems. They will be comfortable respecting divergent opinions, finding consensus, and making our systems work for everyone. Instead of one competing against many, it is many working together as one."

Dave: "Just when I thought ours was a new way of thinking, a friend in California sent this manifesto reputed to be from John Wesley in the 18th century. There is a note that modern believers have updated his words and thoughts, but the ideas are good even if he didn't say exactly this:

1. Reduce the gap between rich people and poor people
2. Help everyone to have a job
3. Help the poorest, including a living wage
4. Offer the best possible education
5. Help everyone to feel they can make a difference

6. Promote tolerance
7. Promote the equal treatment of women
8. Create a society based on values and not on profits and consumerism
9. End all forms of slavery
10. Avoid getting into wars
11. Share the love of God with everyone
12. Care for the environment.

"I guess we can add another 21st century update to this.

13. Encourage cooperative behavior
14. Focus education on critical thinking and the application of knowledge to solve real problems
15. Use positive reinforcement and not competitive and negative feedback like that gained from standardized models
16. Identify people as people, not by gender, race, wealth, family position, or political power

"Pretty great don't you think?"

Mr. K: "I want to reiterate what Michael Fullan wrote about new drivers:

1. Well-being and Learning (essence)
2. Social Intelligence (limitless)
3. Equality Investments (dignity)
4. Systemness (wholeness)

"I think we all now understand where he is pointing and it's where we want to be."

Dan: "Mr. K, that says it all. Now we can go on to . . . where do we go from here? Dave, what are you thinking?"

Dave: "I'm trying to understand how we got the education system we have. I'm trying to comprehend our Western viewpoint that builds an education approach that ignores Wesley's wisdom. I think I know the answer, but I don't like it. The industrial revolution is a machine age that still exploits human beings. Those who developed that economic system wanted conformed workers who were not trained to think independently, who were interchangeable and who would not rise up and demand the basic things that make life tolerable like decent working hours and payment for their sweat equity. Those who shaped education to fit that economic system were willing to create slaves—a partially educated worker class that could be used, abused, and deprived of the fruits of their labor. Everything became a commodity to be bought, sold, and hoarded."

Ron: "I agree with you Dave, and we are still suffering today from that economic philosophy. Most who control the U.S. economic system still abuse labor. Some things are better, but take healthcare as an example. All advanced western cultures provide universal healthcare as a human right. All but one. The United States. And look at the battles going on with those who intend to destroy public education. They definitely want to stop those who are educated from changing the system of greed and power. Creeps like the members of the Koch family, the Mercers, the DeVos clan, and ALEC people who call themselves Libertarians, have done everything they can to maintain a system where they benefit from the labor of others and have unhindered access to public resources. There's nothing truly libertarian about it, just vulture capitalism that exploits until it breaks something and then runs to the taxpayers for the bailouts they condemned."

George: "Ron, you hit on something I became aware of recently. Fred Koch, the father of Charles and David was one of the founders of the John Birch Society. I read their tenets: destroy public education, privatize prisons, and destroy any form of worker organization like unions. The Society may have changed their public face, but those who are working to those ends have had amazing success. They have tentacles into every level of education, every State Department of Education, every university, and every state legislature. They have been successful in starving public education and then devising ways to show that the starved schools are failing. They are working to destroy the federal unification of education, and look what they have been able to do. We have just exited four years of control of the U.S. Department of Education by a person who is tragically ignorant, who comes from a racist family that wants to destroy public schools which encourage critical thinking, and more.

"Just look at how this group has tread over indigenous land rights. Pipeline rights-of-way and contaminated watersheds are just the tip of the iceberg. Look at their record of withdrawing protection from public lands so they can rape them for their own personal gain using the corporations they control. How about their work to support Trump's failed vanity wall on the Mexican border? How about the proposed foreign development of a massive copper mine on indigenous land in Arizona? And they reach so deep into our culture that almost half of the population are convinced they should be fighting against their own best interests."

Claire: "The Civics curriculum in most of our schools is written by extreme anti-public education right wing groups like The American Legislative Executive Council (ALEC). It is an anti-representative, anti-democratic group of over two-thousand members who have infiltrated state governments. It is funded by the people you mentioned, Ron. Legislators are bribed with free trips to posh resorts where they are given model legislation to introduce in their state to promote the libertarian, anti-regulation, anti-government agenda. Under the guise of false patriotism, they are working diligently to undermine every effort to build a unified, integrated, tolerant and well-educated America. They control many charitable 501 (C)(3) organizations. Subversives are also designing a civics program for the future, iCivics, which is intended to convert students to their way of thinking without the public even knowing about it."

Ron: "Claire, how do you know about that? I mean what's your source?"

Claire: "I first learned about this subversion when we were researching *Human Competence*. Remember Dan, we all came to that understanding. What I learned then was confirmed by Diane Ravitch in her blog: *A Warning: Who Is Paying For Your State's Civics*

Courses? Jan 3, 2021.' A few days later I got this from Diane Ravitch's blog of January 8, 2021:

> As educators, we must remember that the first obligation of public schools is to develop good citizens. Not compliant citizens, not indoctrinated citizens, but citizens who are knowledgeable about our government and our institutions; citizens who can weigh evidence, listen to opposing views, and think critically about their decisions. We need citizens who can tell the difference between facts and propaganda."

Ken: "Claire, that's exactly the kind of competency we are saying we need to develop, especially if kids will be forced to confront a future where lying may be valued more than truth. Students will definitely need critical thinking skills to evaluate this overwhelming abundance of false information."

Mary: "Roberto, what are we missing as we think of the future of education? It seems like most every problem that the U.S. has now is related to education systems designed to enslave, not free people. If a student is lucky enough to get a teacher that is not perpetuating the lies, they are taught to verify sources, check facts, and they quickly start to identify the Koch-ALEC agenda as the propaganda it is. But, then they feel betrayed by the system and many feel they need to step out of it, or replace it—confusing the exploitation of these groups with the power and value of the system itself."

Roberto: "It's true Mary. I learned how to get information and check it. I moved ahead seeking some truth about what was happening in America. I had focused on war and I decided that war was used as a tool to retain power, control resources, and operate without government regulation. As I studied, I learned that those in power in the 19th century wanted an education system that not only trained semi-skilled labor but also willing soldiers. They did not want an educated populous strong enough to oppose them. At least, not for everyone outside their small group of white males. The education systems they devised taught the 3 Rs, and conformed the masses. Is it any wonder that people with this same mentality promote standardized models now? George, you studied this in depth."

George: "Let me share what I learned about our history. By the beginning of the twentieth century, through reformers like Teddy Roosevelt, followed by the trust busters, the Sherman Anti-trust Act, the Great Depression, and Franklin Roosevelt; the so-called great industrialists were brought under a modicum of control. Following WW II, there was an amazing period where a middle class emerged. In 1957, Sputnik caused us to look at science and a catch-up mentality existed that brought us into the space age. But forces using the actor Ronald Reagan, feared the rise of a middle class which took wealth they felt was their own. Since Reagan's time, advances in social programs and human issues have been carved away. It is inconceivable that when Reagan decided to tax social security—remember, we are already taxed on the income we paid into social security—too many liked this actor puppet and supported him. Some even believed in trickle-down economics. The end result we deal with today? The middle class lost ground and the 1% pocketed their wealth. The future of social security and people's hard earned investment money is in danger. Social security probably won't even exist for us.

"The record is clear. The vulture libertarians began to starve public schools and stop any advances they made. The creation of competitive 'public' charter schools has been used to erode public education; to take away the threat posed to them by an educated populous. Meanwhile, instead of funding children's educations—OUR education—the money is funneled into tax schemes and rent-for-profit schemes that pad the pockets of these investors. I'm all for people making a bit of a profit if they bring innovation and build value. But these? These people erode and sap value. They siphon off huge sums of money and resources at the cost of the very people they're supposed to be helping. It's like the snake oil salesmen of the last century selling lies and preying on people's desire to do good and improve things. Sorry about the lecture . . . it just makes me so mad."

Susan: "Yes, but remember, through all of this turmoil and change, exceptional teachers made important in-roads into modes of instruction."

Mary: "You mean the certified and experienced teachers that haven't been driven out. But we can't forget that schools were still focused on competition, conformity, reading, writing and arithmetic. American History and Civics classes lauded the political system and the idea of checks and balances between the three branches of government, and rightly so. But too many schools taught interpretations of the Constitutional system which favored corporations. Eventually corporations were given human rights. Citizen's rights were weakened or ignored. Or, they taught nothing about government, history and civics. This was most prevalent in charter schools where there is little accountability. They intentionally ignored, as the Zinn Education Project has so clearly pointed out, that understanding our actual American history is necessary if we are to prepare students to make positive social change. Truth telling vs. lies."

Claire: "I learned that there were enlightening surges in the late 60s when voter rights, human rights, healthcare, and social safety nets were major issues driving society. But the system kept students ignorant of the issues that affect them. The schools were not preparing students to work together to solve problems—problems those in power didn't want solved. I now believe that our schools create citizens who work and vote against their own best interests."

Frank: "Hey I think we should move on to a slightly different topic. I'm concerned about classes that are so large that a teacher can't work with the students effectively. I spent a year in a multi-age classroom. They combined kids from 3 grades. There were sixty kids and 1 teacher. It was chaos. The teacher tried to group kids according to ability but there were too many of us. Then add untrained, inexperienced teachers into the mix who have no idea about what it takes to control a classroom, teach subjects, meet individual student needs, or be part of a profession. It was such a waste of our time. There were just too many students in every class."

Roberto: "I was thinking about this too, Frank. In grades 9 through 12, I think the ideal class would have under fifteen students. But most of the teachers lectured so that thirty or more desks were filled. When budgets got tight, there could be up to forty-five. Once in a while we broke into groups, but we were not cooperating, just following the directions the teacher gave us. At the university, there are freshman classes of over four hundred students."

Mary: "Same at my school. When they broke us into groups, only a few of us did the work, and the other kids coasted."

George: "Other kids? You mean kids who were not part of the 'in' group, like Ken, Roberto and me . . . and girls who were not popular because their parents were poor or something? I hated groups. We always got dumped on and were looked at as losers. It was much harder to fade into the background and hide."

Annie: "By the time students get to 6th grade, the damage has already been done. If they didn't learn prejudice and intolerance in school, they learned it from their parents. Maybe humans are just inherently tribal, and we can't bridge differences and work through our fears of the 'other.' It's that privileged people bit."

Susan: "Maybe . . . but kids take their cues from adults and too many adults are not aware of the signals they send. A teacher who sees black kids as trouble makers, or an African American teacher who is competitive with Hispanics or Mexicans, gives a subliminal kind of permission to perpetuate hate in the classroom. Sensitivity training should be an important part of teacher training, especially for elementary school teachers. We need to provide tools to teachers to identify and reflect on their own prejudices, so they can overcome them and create positive spaces for all kids. There's not a human alive that doesn't have some sort of bias . . . including us! We're talking though."

Mary: "Susan, I'm thinking what we need to do is identify the need for teachers to communicate positive acceptance of every kid. And that may be easy. If a kid is disruptive, or even mentally challenged, the teacher has to have the professional skills to turn the situation into a positive encounter and to redirect that energy. You know, I think most teachers in the early grades do this all the time. But I think some teachers, especially in the upper grades, use reaction and rejection as a means of control. And then there is the new concept of uncertified 'warm bodies' that can be placed in classrooms and called teachers. We all know what happens to kids under their control."

Frank: "And I thought we had it at the first try. We talked a lot about this in our first campfires. Okay, to change education we have to reinforce what most teachers already know. They are role models. If they have problems with certain types of kids, they need to get over them or be fired. This is the type of thing that scars kids for life. Several of us have already touched on that. I think someone mentioned grouping kids by ability and maturity and other things that may make it difficult for them to participate in a normal group. Maybe it would make it easier if you were not having to compete so much."

Mary: "I wonder if that would result in some type of tracking. I remember when my school did that. We had the elite and the dumbbells."

Susan: "No Mary, good experienced teachers don't do that. They believe that every student is gifted and that it is their job to know the child well enough to help her participate. I worked as an aide in an elementary school and I saw teachers do this. Sure, they worked with the students who were way behind in small groups or individually, but they weren't labeled. The teacher worked with all the kids in this way. These teachers knew there were at least ten types of intelligences, and many levels of maturity."

Annie: "Okay so we are not introducing something new. Real certified teachers, and especially elementary school teachers, get to know each child and work him or her into the class. The few kids who come into the class who are not ready—kids from homes where they were never read to or involved as part of a healthy family, and kids with ACE—adverse childhood experiences that are so traumatized that they cannot learn, are not put aside. When possible, they are introduced into the group and allowed to participate. The idea is to build on strengths, not weaknesses. If these children need special help and would not be able to participate without damaging other children, they must have special care and treatment that only trained professionals can give."

Roberto: "Annie, everyone, the concept of building collaborative groups who work together to solve problems is possible. If that continues up through the grades it completely changes education. It empowers students, increases networking, and broadens power to break up the top-down authoritative model."

George: "Hey, it's late and I'm sure you are all thinking about holiday plans. We can get back together after the holidays. Doc, can we decide on a date? Can everybody gather around the campfire a week from next Tuesday? Do you have a problem, Dan? Are there conflicts with Chinese holidays?"

Dan: "No conflict. I'm trying to get my mind wrapped around all that we have talked about. I realize I have no idea about the curriculum for the future. Do schools still teach Science the way they did a few years ago? What about History? What about Art? If SI is a brain patterned after ours, but millions of times faster and more efficient, I'd like to get back to identifying what kids should be learning to partner with it?

"I'm trying to understand and it would help me if we started the next campfire with insights into what we need. I know I need time right now to gather more information. I'm listening to YouTube interviews with Yuval Noah Harari. And I want to find out what Dr. Martin has to say about the future. I need to do research, clarify my thinking, and digest all this new information. We all do."

George: "Hey all, hold it right here. I'm not ready to move forward. I realize that I don't understand what it means when we say 'curriculum'. Doc you spent time studying schools in the USA and twenty-two countries around the world, what did you look for? How did you evaluate what schools did or didn't do?"

Doc: "Curricula on the K-12 level is the student's introduction to the world we live in. Curricula must be designed so that it exposes students to a broad spectrum of information and thought processes. It is the enemy of myopic thinking.

"We must have comprehensive schools. Schools that are interdisciplinary and teach interwoven subjects that range from anthropology to zoology. Students must have these experiences so that they have a deeper understanding of the world around them and life's options.

"Curriculums are lacking in many schools where ethics, economy, the US Constitution, environmental studies, geography including diverse cultures, accurate history, structural racism, the arts, communication, government, science, computer skills, technology, community service, politics, religions of the world, ecology, truth vs. disinformation, critical thinking, tolerance, and sex education are not being taught.

"I developed a system where I identified specific things that would help me know if a school was working for kids and not just a warehouse used for social control. I wanted to know if the curriculum in the early grades was the foundation for the following grades. Did each grade's curriculum focus on what had been taught and what followed at the next level?

"The ideal curriculum is one where every teacher can explain how what is introduced to students fits into the concepts and activities that are designed to widen the child's options in life; concepts that are enlarged year-by-year, course-by-course. Guided in this way, the child's understanding of the world expands and they have choices and new ways of thinking that they might not have known. The purpose of the K-12 curricula is not to create majors, specialists, or workers, but to introduce students to the widest possibilities available for them.

"In higher education, the student can specialize and focus on interests. By that time, if the K-12 curricula prepared them properly, they would have multiple options and an appreciation for other ways of thinking.

"That is why partial schools, like charter, voucher, and all schools with limited curricula cheat students. Schools forced to cut out courses due to financial restrictions placed upon them by so-called 'libertarian legislatures' and those who plan to destroy public schools, damage our nation by dumbing down the citizenry.

"Whenever I visited a school that had to eliminate courses like physical and cultural geography, local, state and federal government (civics), art, music, history, theater, debate, home economics, crafts, wood shop, auto shop, clubs, and/or athletics, I knew the students were graduating without a comprehensive introduction to and understanding of how our complex society works. Students can't participate successfully in our economy or government, if they are uninformed due to limited exposure to a broad-based curriculum.

"The number of courses offered in a comprehensive secondary school is greater than individual students can study. Therefore, in high school there is some tracking and alignment due to student aptitudes and interests. Students who excel in music, science, math, social studies, or languages, etc., are directed to courses that are a good fit. However, *every* student should be exposed to many other ways of thinking, communicating, and learning before they are graduated. There may be whole subject areas that they might not pursue otherwise. Schools with partial curricula that introduce students to limited or focused studies do a great deal of harm."

Chapter 8

Changing the Focus and Methods of Teaching

Claire: "Dan, you gave me something to do between campfires. I took time to research about curriculum. What I learned is that, on a similar level to where we are now, education had to change to fit new advances in technology. Most everything I read from twenty years ago was about students at the grocery store and in cafes that couldn't even make accurate change after a sale. Self-appointed reformers screamed that the schools where failing. Teachers were failing. Other countries had young students who had basic skills. The reformers said that American schools didn't prepare kids to do the most basic things. They were not being prepared for jobs and their futures were . . .

"Well, most of us are aware that today we read similar outcries from those who want to profit from education and gain access to the billions of dollars each year that taxpayers pay for education. Were they right then? Are they right now? Look at where these students are today. Now no one could give a fig about a cashier's ability to make change. A cashier just has to find the USB code on the article, run it through the scanner, and after all the items are checked, run the machine that prints out the bill. If, and this seldom happens, the customer pays in cash, the cashier reads the bill, puts in the amount of cash paid, and the machine tells him how much change is due. Today the machines even dispense the change without the cashier ever having to open the drawer. Even a café or store that does not have sophisticated tech systems has a cash register that can add."

Roberto: "I spent a lot of time searching for examples of curricula. I did find a science curriculum that dealt with AI and access to computer software that could do complicated things like graph changes. I found a few math teachers who were aware that Einstein's brain is now part of advanced thinking which will be done by super computers. Most of the curricula for science and math is focused on teaching the foundations, the basics. I kept looking for evidence that teachers were figuring out what not to teach. You know, like in Dan's example, things that will be done by computers that students don't need to know. What do you think, Susan? Why are you smiling?"

Susan: "I came to similar conclusions, Roberto. What not to teach is a key. That's not an easy task. We are already behind. I do believe that even complex and advanced machines that far surpass what any single human or even a group of humans can do, can serve us. But we have to change the way we think and the way we assume the world works.

"We have identified what it is to be human. We think we know what it is to be a machine. The problem is, we are not teaching humans to build their human skills. We keep wanting to train everyone for a worldview mired in the past. The Periodic Table of Elements is an amazing insight into chemistry. Can super computers use it for us? I mean, do we need to memorize it? Do people need to learn it or is SI like having a great teacher working for us who knows all of this stuff and can do what we would do if we could? The answer I came up with is that most of us cannot understand Einstein, but we will benefit from his work because it is embedded in SI and that advances who we are.

"We are searching for why? We just burst out of the top of the tipi. We are defining our species as it evolves and must continue to change. We are shedding our mental skins and emerging—our metamorphosis. We are not yet butterflies, but we have created tools like super computers that free us from non-productive activity. This allows us to focus our productivity on improving the health and well-being of all species on the planet. We can fulfill our potential as beings worthy of a role in the universe. We see and hear all of the ugly things our species does to each other and to the environment. We have behaviors that destroy life and will end us if we continue to do them. That answers the question. Why? Because we must change or we will not be a species that survives."

Roberto: "Beautifully said Susan. All the thinking I did over the break was focused on things we teach. We still need basic skills but the focus and content will be very different. Are there subjects we teach in school now that will still benefit us in the next stage of our evolution? Is mastering basic skills a process that prepares kids for learning other jobs? There are things we may teach that will help mankind. How we communicate with one another and share ideas will probably be very different. I thought Fullan's ideas about 'drivers' was pretty impressive. I especially liked his work, *A Guide for School Leaders*."

Ken: "Yes, and Frank let's be honest and realistic. Humanity is not ready to exit the tipi. Some may be, but they are few. We still say, 'All men are created equal', and too many know that we don't mean women, or people of color, or people who adapted to equatorial latitudes. We still hold the conqueror mentality that everything is there for the taking; it is okay to destroy or enslave entire populations and cultures because we want what they have and we have the advantage. We still have types of slavery. We are always at the brink of, or in wars. Too many white people think they are superior to people with brown or black skin. They are just starting to realize they are people of color too, and the balance is shifting. We have children going hungry in the wealthiest country on Earth. We raise, kill and eat other animals who often die suffering violent deaths and emotional trauma in slaughterhouses. The oceans of the world are endangered by over fishing and plastic waste. The rain forests are already so damaged that the CO_2 oxygen cycle is no longer working to replenish our air. The planet's top soils are almost gone, and it is predicted that we have less than sixty years of harvests left. All of these atrocities can be corrected. We have the intelligence to change things, but do we have the common will? It is a pretty intimidating prospect don't you think?"

Frank: "Yes Ken, what you say is true. And I

know you well enough now to understand that you don't believe we shouldn't try. We have to face reality and we have to work to change things we can. Sometimes there is an event, or an invention, or an idea that can make global change quickly. Look at how the pandemic rocked the world. Widespread virtual education became a reality within a few months. Suddenly people, young and old, were using Zoom. A lot of students and families also learned that they really missed the social connection of in-person learning. We have seen that it is possible to make change in a hurry if there is a compelling reason. Awareness of SI is growing. People recognize we are living in a world where technology is integrated into everything. It is a new age and the old industrial model is dead."

Roberto: "I've been kinda quiet around the campfire this evening and what is being discussed is giving me head cramps. Over the break I was digging around and found this guy, John Spencer. He is Assistant Professor of Education at George Fox University, west of me over in Oregon. He writes that he is, '. . . on a quest to transform schools into bastions of creativity and wonder. I want to see teachers unleash the creative potential in all of their students so that kids can be makers, designers, artists, and engineers. I explore research, interview educators, deconstruct systems, and study real-world examples of design thinking in action.' He has a list of seven things that need to be done in our schools. I think these are competencies we should consider:

1. Focus on values rather than rules.

Too often, students end up in what Phillip Schlecty describes as 'ritual compliance,' where they follow the rules in order to get the grade and move on. Adam Grant points out that many of the most innovative thinkers in our world internalized a set of values and ethics that transcended compliance to rules. In other words, parents and teachers encouraged children to ask the 'why' questions and develop a deeper understanding of systems and ideas rather than simply asking, 'what am I supposed to do?'

As a teacher, a shift toward values might include classroom values and concepts rather than strict rules. It might mean designing flexible environments with fewer required procedures. It might mean allowing students to interrupt the scheduled lesson, take a journey down a rabbit trail, and ultimately search for meaning by questioning answers as often as they answer questions.

I know this approach drives my current students (pre-service teachers) crazy. 'How long does this need to be?' Long enough to get your point across. 'Is this right?' Does it seem right to you? 'What is the right way to do this?' Figure out your own way.

Too often, students end their time in school as compliant students rather than critical thinkers. They are afraid of doing things the wrong way. They adopt certain practices that they have been told are the 'right way' (like the five-paragraph essay) without asking why something is right or wrong.

2. Encourage creative risk-taking.

Students don't grow into original thinkers by learning a lesson on how to be original. Instead, it happens when they keep taking creative risks. This is why it helps to treat mistakes as iterations in the creative process. In design thinking, creative risk-taking is a built-in part of the entire process. Students know that 'dumb ideas' are allowed in the Navigate Ideas phase and they recognize that mistakes will happen when they approach the Testing and Revising stage.

Unfortunately, schools tend to punish creative risk-taking. The traditional grading system rewards speed and accuracy by averaging scores. Teachers tend to provide very concrete, specific instructions for how to accomplish a task without allowing wiggle room for creative thinking. However, when teachers encourage and allow creative risk-taking, students grow confident as makers and creative thinkers.

3. Allow for procrastination.

Okay, perhaps procrastination is an over-statement. There is value in creating and sticking to deadlines. However, as Grant points out in 'Originals', many original thinkers need a certain cognitive slack to incubate great ideas.

In my own experience, I tend to have an incubation period of 4-5 months before starting a project. This is where I'm letting an idea sit. For example, my son pitched that crazy superhero taco idea back in January and then I finally wrote the first draft in April. AJ Juliani and I hashed out an idea of a personalized professional development platform. We finally started creating it in March.

This hibernation period is important when people are trying to create something new. However, this can be challenging to pull off in schools. Many schools have rigid curriculum maps and specific benchmark testing. We tend to view late work as a discipline issue. I get it. Deadlines are important. Creative types need to learn the art of getting crap done. And yet . . . what would it mean to create these hibernation periods? What would it look like to incorporate a little more procrastination?

4. Ask.

Often the most original work you do happens when you are 'drafted'. We tend to think of successful creators as natural go-getters who boldly blaze a trail. However, more often than not, they are asked to do something. They are sometimes reluctant at first. And yet, they gain creative confidence when someone else notices creative potential in them. After all, Michelangelo didn't volunteer to paint the Sistine Chapel. In fact, he literally ran away when they first approached him.

This is why relationships are so critical in creative classrooms. Although students should pursue their own areas of passion and purpose, sometimes they need to be noticed in order to take that first big step toward original work. As teachers we can scout out these opportunities and encourage students to make the creative jump into a new project.

5. Be flexible.

Original thinkers tend to be flexible thinkers. They are willing to approach a problem with a different method. They view each approach as an experiment that will inform their next approach. Often what you think you're going to do doesn't end up being what you do—and that's a good thing. Some of the greatest inventions began in one area and evolved into something entirely different.

In design thinking, students typically begin with a clear picture about what they want to create for their audience. However, as they go through the phases of asking questions, learning about the process and the problem, and ultimately navigating ideas, their design concept changes dramatically.

This can be a challenge in a one-size-fits-all standardized school. Too often, we ask students to change in order to fit the system rather than adapting our systems to fit each student. However, creative teachers know how to incorporate choice and agency into their lessons. Their own flexibility allows students to adapt and experiment and modify on their own.

6. Encourage students to follow their curiosity.

In other words, make for the sake of making. For all the talk of empathy as the starting point in design thinking, some of the greatest creative work started out with a simple curiosity. They only truly figured out the audience once they started making. So, a student notices something and that sparks a sense of wonder. The wonder leads to questions and research and over time this leads to original thinking.

This is what I meant in my last post when I mentioned that kindergartners are natural researchers. They know the joy of chasing questions for no other purpose than to chase the questions. This doesn't always look like originality. I've written before, that students often go through stages from consuming to creating. And, honestly, I think this was a bit of a blind spot in Grant's book. All artists are copycats until one day they're not.

But this is all the more reason that schools need to help students become better consumers. It's why classrooms should be filled with awe and wonder and imagination. There are little things we can do at any age. We can let students choose their own topics and books and resources. We can create moments of wonder by allowing for meaningful confusion in science classrooms. We can treat math problems as experiments rather than recipes. We can let kids make and tinker and invent.

7. Be open about the emotional elements of making.

One of the big take-aways from the

book is the fact that so many of the creative geniuses I admire essentially hedged their bets. They were terrified before they launched their work. They avoided work because they were afraid that they wouldn't ever be good enough. As teachers, we can reduce the fear of creative failure by leading discussions about the emotional side of creative work. We can conference with students so that students feel safe sharing their fears. We can share our own creative struggles as teacher-makers. We can change the assessment policies so that we aren't punishing mistakes. And we can remind students that their creative heroes are just as terrified as they are.

Final Thoughts:

These ideas run against the current climate of education. However, in a world of no-nonsense 'high standards', and an incessant focus on 'grit,' we can provide an alternative approach. We can give slack. We can be open. We can let students play around with ideas. We can experiment. We can be original.

"What do you think everyone? Seems like everything he wrote is right in line with our thinking and the ideas we have been exploring about human competence. I don't know his opinions on cooperative work. Most of these qualities are under the self-actualization part which Maslow, in his hierarchy of needs, puts as the end goal. We talked about how the Blackfoot Confederation puts self-actualization at the beginning—the base of the triangle which is the start of where we need to be. Do you agree Ken?"

Ken: "Sorry Roberto. I had to read it through and then think about it. Yes, I agree. I can begin to envision approaches that build human competence. Originality. I really like that. Thanks Roberto."

George: "All of Spencer's stuff really makes sense to me. By encouraging students to live and breathe the creative process, the human strengths outlined by Spencer, they are being prepared to live in the future and have the skills to utilize SI as a tool without being controlled by it. Shifting the emphasis from regimentation to creativity will prepare students for the tasks ahead.

"I'm thinking that computers can simulate music and create music, their own genre of music perhaps, but can even the 'smartest' computer on the planet be curious? Can it follow any course where data doesn't lead? Can it truly create? Does it have the capacity to love, be emotional, have empathy? With data, I assume a computer intelligence can be critical. But can it engage in critical thinking—critical thought? Can a computer understand universal basic human income from both data analyses and human needs? Can we trust machine intelligence to make decisions that enhance or limit human suffering? YES, probably in economic terms, but NO, I don't think so in people terms. Ron, what did you find?"

Ron: "I was reading some of Dr. Katie Martin's materials. I liked *Challenging the Status Quo to Rewrite New School Rules*. I think her ideas fit here.

> When you are so used to a compliance-driven model it is often hard to imagine that kids (and all people) can function outside of a control and command environment because we are so used to how people operate in our existing systems. When I bring educators to visit the schools that are challenging the status quo, they are always struck by the culture of care and agency rather than control. High school students

> have meetings off-campus, connect with mentors and work on projects in hospital and board rooms. Students are using tools, building houses, writing code, and starting movements in their communities and beyond. Early elementary school kids are allowed to choose seats, get a drink of water, and even move freely in and out of the classroom. Kids are celebrated and coached to make good choices not scolded, trained, and managed."

Dave: "Sounds like a school I would like to attend. In his course intro, Doc says that as a young idealist he spent a year in twenty-two countries asking questions about their education systems. He believed that we could predict the future of a country by the way they educate their children. Well, I just spent a good part of three weeks searching for groups that are specifically preparing students to deal with SI, the new player on Planet Earth. I didn't have much luck. Spencer and Martin have great observations. Anybody else?"

Claire: "Dave, while I think there is very little information out there, as I was snorkeling around and searched on the 'future of learning', I found this quote from Stephen Johnson, April 16, 2020 in an article: *New AI Improves Itself Through Darwinian-style Evolution*:

> Automatic machine learning is a fast-developing branch of deep learning. It seeks to vastly reduce the amount of human input and energy needed to apply machine learning to real-world problems.
>
> AutoML-Zero, developed by scientists at Google, serves as a simple proof-of-concept that shows how this kind of technology might someday be scaled up and applied to more complex problems. Machine learning has fundamentally changed how we engage with technology. Today, it's able to curate social media feeds, recognize complex images, drive cars down the interstate, and even diagnose medical conditions, to name a few tasks. But while machine learning technology can do some things automatically, it still requires a lot of input from human engineers to set it up and point it in the right direction. Inevitably, that means human biases and limitations are baked into the technology.

"Reminds me of the profound contrast between the 'good' android Data, and his 'malevolent' brother Lore, in *Star Trek's Next Generation* series."

Dave: "I remember those characters. So, it seems to me human biases can be a good thing or a bad thing depending on intent . . . that phrase 'pointing it in the right direction' seems significant. What if scientists could minimize their influence on the process by creating a system that generates its own machine-learning algorithms? Could it discover new solutions that humans have never considered?"

Claire: "Think about it George. This is like confirming that computers can self-learn and self-teach. If machines can learn through the analysis of data, is that different than what we expect students to learn as directed by standardized tests which are used to teach a common core of data?"

Ron: "George, Annie, everybody. I was searching all kinds of programs and . . . Hey, what's going on . . . is someone hacking into our campfire? Hold on everyone. Claire, Doc, are we getting hacked? Dave, do you know someone named Chan Bandy? He wants in. Says you contacted him."

Dave: "Me? I don't think I know him."

Chan: "I'm not a hacker. Dave, remember when you were searching on Detroit schools a while back? My name is Chan, Chan Bandy. I'm not a teacher but I'm being used as a substitute teacher for the Detroit middle schools. I'm just nineteen and want to go to college to become a teacher. I got hired because I'm male and black and they thought I could relate to middle school kids."

Dave: "Detroit? I did spend some time trying to understand what happened to your schools. I was researching what Betsy DeVos did to Michigan, not just her but others; and about the lead and copper poisoning. You were on that site too?"

Chan: "I was. I also read *Human Competence* when I was searching for information about education and ways to improve the system. Several friends recommended it. I want in your campfire group—not because I disagree with what you are doing, but because I am concerned by what you are not including."

Claire: "We've already been underway for several months, Chan, but we are eager for new perspectives. Please tell us a bit more about yourself."

Chan: "I'm very protective about telling people about my heritage, but here goes. I'm a person of color and that has influenced almost every aspect of my life. My skin is very dark. I'm part black, part Hispanic, and part white man in the woodpile. I get around all of that here in Detroit because everybody underrates me. I get work because I'm willing to go into the war zones. You know, I mean middle schools, right? I read, I think, I analyze, I am good at seeing the broader picture, and I try to communicate in ways that are respectful of diversity. I think I have some good insights to share as a substitute teacher and I definitely am interested in transforming public schools to be relevant to students in the future. Can I join you?"

Annie: "Okay by me, Chan. Raise your hand everyone if you would like to admit Chan into the group. . . . Looks like you are in. Welcome to the campfires, Chan. I'm Annie."

Frank: "Okay let's continue. Chan you said you wanted to share your perspective on what we are missing. Fire away."

Chan: "Nothing like diving right in. Well, what I'm wrestling with is what happens if we stop teaching the basics."

Ron: "Hi, I'm Ron. Why would anyone stop teaching kids the basics? Is this happening in Detroit? Did we do or say something that led you to believe that we advocate doing away with the basics; the foundations? We are talking about the way teachers can enhance cooperation and collaboration, teamwork, creative problem solving, mutual respect and more. Part of what we are shifting is content to make it better suited to a future of integrated tech, and part of it is emphasis and structure. We have no problem with teaching the basics in every grade and class. I think we're all in agreement on that."

Chan: "This is the problem I'm facing as I try to help kids in our schools. Every curriculum, every test, is geared to the assumption that a student is a failure if she can't pass a sixth-grade test in reading or math. Reading we can agree is essential, but not all kids read at a certain grade level or age. Math is an aptitude. Some kids have it, some don't. Basic arithmetic is essential. Writing, well we used to think cursive writing skills were essential. Try to explain to an 80s teacher why texting with your thumbs has replaced learning to type on machines that are almost extinct now. Vocal commands are taking over most communications with machines. Students ask SIRI or ALEXA to look up information, add, multiply, subtract, or divide. I know you talked about 'what not to teach', but they test and grade students on proficiency in only two disciplines as if that is an accurate way to define their success in life. The results of these standardized tests are also being used to evaluate teacher and school performance, as if all kids, classrooms, and schools are created equal."

Ron: "Chan, the mastery of skills the kids will need for their future is not measured on tests used throughout our school systems. I . . . we have been working to design a system that will allow people to build on their individual strengths without the need to memorize information that is readily accessible using SI; to work collaboratively within teams; to re-frame the goal of education from standardization to creative thinking. Passing or failing tests is irrelevant. Most importantly, we are searching for others who see a need to change the paradigm away from the system that has been in place for 200 years. We don't still use a horse and wagon for transportation, or a telegraph for every day communication. Why would we keep using the same system of education we have had for two centuries? Technology has changed the world and there is no going back. We need to evolve. By the way. Where in the blazes are you? It sounds like you're in an echo chamber and what's all that noise?"

Chan: "I had hoped to have video, but the signal is too weak here. I'm in a McDonalds not far from downtown. They stay open until eleven and then I have to get out. The middle school principal here supports what I am doing and is trying to find a way I can use his office and WiFi. Our district infrastructure is pretty limited. Originally you guys all had avatars. Why did you stop?"

Mary: "We stopped when we were not afraid of being identified. You can invent one if it helps, but we all decided that we wanted to know each other. I'm Mary, by the way."

George: "Hey Chan, I'm George. During our original campfires in *Human Competence*, I had chosen a white male avatar to avoid prejudice. I never felt comfortable in that guy's 'skin', so I am happy here in *Imperatives* to be accepted for the real me. Here at the campfire, we have developed a trust and honesty that we all value. I bring in viewpoints that others might not have and vice versa. In this group I've never been discounted. If you get involved and work with us to solve problems, you will be a fellow human being.

"Chan, everybody, I want to share with the group something that happened when I watched the presidential inauguration ceremonies. A twenty-three-year-old lady came up to the podium. She was introduced as America's National Youth Poet Laureate, Amanda Gorman. Personally, I was already in a state of joy, as Kamala Harris made history as both the first woman, and a woman from an Asian and black family background, to become Vice President. Then this powerful young black woman took to the podium and began to read her poem. I have read and listened again to Amanda's stunning poem. I'm sure you have too. But the thoughts that went through my head were about her—where did she come from? How did she get the support to be part of this inauguration? How did she make it through the public schools? What was her education like? When she goes to Harvard, what will the snobs and privileged system do to her?

"I did a bit of research and read that she had attended the New Roads School in California. I Googled and fell heart and mind into their world. I hope you will all do the same. I think we have found another important example of a strong education model for the future.

> We the people of New Roads liberate young individuals through the pursuit of justice, equity, and opportunity; raising generations of powerfully compassionate advocates in an intellectual habitat driven

> by authentic diversity—ultimately empowering them to disrupt systems that produce inequality and build a more just future.
>
> Intellectual Rigor, Activism, Diverse Advantage, Equity, Well-being. Inspired Pedagogy.
>
> We the People of New Roads were made for this moment—it's why we were founded as a school. Solidarity and allyship are in our DNA. And we will continue to educate and liberate our youth to build a more equitable tomorrow."

Dan: "Yes! That philosophy seems right in line with what we have been saying. She is a perfect example of how the school adapted to her needs and she flourished; touching millions of lives with her poem, passion, skill, creativity and artistry. What's up, Ron?"

Ron: "I found someone else I want to share as I searched for AI-SI information on the Internet, in magazines, listening to TED Talks, and dozens of other sources. I found a podcast about a book by Max Tegmark, an MIT scholar, that got my attention. I ordered his book, *Life 3.0: Being Human In The Age of Artificial Intelligence*. When it came, I started reading and wow, it blew me away. The only other author that has totally entranced me like him is Yuval Noah Harari. I'm recommending that each of us read Tegmark's book. Read it and especially the preface, 'The Tale of The Omega Team'.

"Max Tegmark's, *Life 3.0*, has clarified the path for those of us who are asking questions about AI-SI and trying to answer them. We want to know, how does a machine made of metal, chips, and plastics, designed and assembled by people, turn intelligent? How can a machine learn? Is it possible for this intelligence to break away from human control and become something beyond our powers to comprehend? How do humans relate to this machine? Is this a creation combining humans and machines as cyborg? If not a cyborg, what exactly is this creation and what drives it? Is this new machine capable of consciousness? Are human beings ready to partner with this new power? Is this the next step in human evolution or is our species doomed? Has our species created a successor which does not need a biological partner?

"Max discusses these things and much more. His book really explores whether humankind is prepared for the future that is already upon us."

Claire: "Looks like that is a good place to stop. The next time we gather will be our last. Doc and Mr. K would like each of us to summarize what we have learned through this process. Pull some thoughts together and we'll meet next week.

"Looking back over all my notes, we've covered a lot of ground in this second campfire series of gatherings. We've found inspiration and faith in the future as we have struggled to fight against fear; to identify the core components of our humanity. We have new ideas about how to structure education, and we have discovered linkages to others along the way who are also fighting for positive change."

Chapter 9

What We Learned at the Campfires

Mr. K: "Welcome everyone to our last meeting. We have explored some pretty heavy-duty topics in our time together. We all gave voice to many of our fears about the future. We questioned the narcissistic intentions of those in power, felt the hopelessness, and made a conscious choice to find a positive path forward.

"With the fast-paced development of sophisticated powerful machine intelligence, our species is facing challenges unlike any we have seen before. If this super intelligence, patterned after our own brains, is amassing data at almost light speed, isn't this a natural process of evolution?

"We have to keep evolving or we will end. We have to adapt or we will not fit in to the times ahead. We have responsibilities to care for each other and to respect our connection with other species. The tipi is open to the sky.

"We have explored a lot of ideas about how to refocus education. Human beings have to move toward inclusion and away from exclusion, otherwise we will continue to sow the seeds of our own destruction as a species. If we change and redefine the qualities we value, then some of us will adapt to a super intelligence and bring the finest human qualities into a more mature and wiser state of being. You give us hope.

"Doc and I have set a stage and we have acted upon it. We ask you to share at least two things that we can include in our second book.

"1) What major things did you learn that will help you prepare for your future?
"2) What major question still remains to be answered?

"Chan, we'll start with you. What have you learned? What conclusions have you drawn?"

Chan: "Geez, last in, first out. Okay I'll start. The campfires have opened a whole new world of self-confidence for me. I can acknowledge that I am important and what I have to say is valued. I can rise above the limitations put on me because of my heritage and other people's bigotry. I can contribute as an equal and grow without limitations. Reading Diane Ravitch's blogs, she introduced me to Dr. Katie Martin, who writes about designing for learners not schools. She describes what we call top-down coercive systems, as control and command environments of compliance that are not favorable to learning. That information cemented my thinking and helped me realize that people like me who don't fit into the system, when freed from the system's controls and commands, accelerate their learning and take charge. I realized that the angry, frustrated, damaged kids in my middle school classes were not helped by traditional modes of teaching. All that system generates is negative energy, frustration, punishment, and failure.

"For the first time, I understand how many schooling approaches destroy creative and positive energy. There is no way kids can make a contribution in most existing schools. In *Human Competence*, Doc introduced us to John Dewey who said that all education must result in a person making a contribution to himself and to society. The campfire meetings have convinced me that if the kids are involved in cooperative problem-solving, they will be empowered to make contributions.

"Many education leaders share a wealth of information in books and other sources. In the future, I'm going to know a lot more about their work. I think sharing sources we find is really helpful and discussing them together is a joy I want and need. That is another thing I learned at the campfires. I will never stop learning and connecting with great people and campfires where people are seeking answers.

"As an untrained stand-in for a substitute teacher in a non-functioning middle school, I am in a pretty daunting situation. I see that many of the frustrated and hurt teachers I have met have their hearts in the right places but they are forced to buy into a model they know does not work for kids. We all know it . . . we see it every day.

"I'm going to work on incorporating viewpoints that allow change through non-coercive and non-competitive systems to serve kids.

"There is something else I am concerned about. There will always be kids who are, for whatever reasons, not ready to work with others and focus on problem solving. I know we didn't address programs for these kids and the teachers who work with them. I am convinced that a non-competitive, outcome-based program for these kids will work to bring them along.

"It remains to be seen what unforeseen events in the near future, much like the global pandemic, will finally force the system to change and adapt."

Annie: "Toto, I'm not in Kansas anymore. We are all in a global society. I joined this campfire because in the *Human Competence* campfires I learned that I am in charge of my own education. In the first campfires, we figured out many strengths we humans have that machines don't have. It was a positive and empowering experience. I joined this campfire open and ready to learn how to prepare students for their future. As I did some prep work I got scared. I picked up a lot of depressing feelings from many sources. In all honesty, those thoughts and feeling have not gone away—they are even stronger now that I am beginning to grasp the power of SI.

"Chan mentioned making a contribution to oneself and to society. This was the first time I was aware that I could be a contributor. In all my schooling, this was the first time I empowered myself to seek out sources of information and apply them. Before that, I only did what I was told to do for a grade.

"My parents assume that our work involves changing what is taught and ordering a new system for inculcating facts. That word inculcate even sounds like brow-beating . . . I love it. I think I have convinced them that we are more interested in how we learn; how we can work together and solve real problems we will face in our future. Together we have identified very human qualities that machines do not have. These competencies are fundamental to a new, evolving curriculum. We are learning how to learn as we master the basics. I try to explain that programming kids like computers and using standardized tests to measure the success of programming should be banned.

"Two years ago, I had no connection with educators and philosophers who were providing their insights into the future of humanity. I could have cared less about the work of Fullan, Harari, Ravitch, Martin, Turner, Novak, Spencer, Tegmark and many others who were putting themselves out there and reaching for people like me. In the present I would not have met these thinkers and leaders. Maybe it will be different at the university, but it does not happen in schools like ours with a standardized curriculum. They are currently designed to teach us how to circle the wagons, not solve problems and work cooperatively to prepare for a future with AI and SI.

"What major question still remains? It scares me, so I'll say it. Does our species have within it the ability and the will to survive? Those who want to destroy public education have succeeded in driving professional and certified teachers out of the profession. They replace them with lower paid temporary stand-ins who have little idea of the problems kids bring with them to school. They have little experience dealing with the stress that blocks learning and cooperation or classroom management. Teaching requires complex knowledge of subjects, human beings, and requires professional training. Our record as humans is good and bad. Does the bad outweigh the balance and eventually end us? I will say, working together around these campfires has kindled a small spark of hope."

George: "Before cosmic forces got me connected via the Internet with Doc and the first campfire, I had mastered survival in school. I had a mask and a fake identity as a student that was so totally focused on war and warfare that I was in a protective bubble. Teachers admired my interests and accumulated knowledge in part, I think, because I was black and exceeded expectations.

"Going virtual and finding anonymity through my avatar gave me more freedom. It didn't come without a price though. I realized in time, I had to be the authentic me. To do that, I had to break out, take the risk, and show myself to be an equal member of the team. You all have helped me gain confidence and I have seen that gender, race, previous education and the judgements used to put people down don't always count. I am slowly moving beyond the games I had to play to survive in the other system.

"Now we are doing another campfire problem-solving session. Only it's not like any class I have ever had. I am hooked into whole new learning experiences, many of my own making. I am reaching out to others and applying their insights into how I think about things. I have learned to see some of my own biases. There are women on our team that make contributions that are accepted if and because they are important insights, without any difference in how they would be accepted and considered if they were men. Hardly a day goes by that I wonder why I had to hide the real 'me' behind a mask. I am always amazed when others share the same awakenings. In our virtual place we created trust and are free to be all that we can be.

"What I learned about AI-SI scares the hell out of me. I don't think I like or trust our species. In my heart of hearts, if I were a judge looking at the human record, I'd rule in favor of extermination. But something is happening to me that I like. I am starting to believe that if we build on human strengths—the good parts—we can evolve and be something beyond what we are now. Like Ken's Blackfoot example, we can change and partner with a purely data-driven intelligence so that it reflects humanity's potential. We can be almost godlike.

"What major question remains to be answered? Will we succeed?"

Susan: "I joined these campfires after reading *Human Competence*. I really support the way the dynamic changed as we, the students, took on the role of researchers and responsibility for our own education.

This was the first time I learned how students could be involved in the process of self-education in a group, team, or class focused on solving real problems.

"When I joined the campfires, I sensed the fear other students had of the future. I sensed it, but could not accept that our species was in trouble. I tried to read all the dystopian views that struck urgency in the hearts of my peers. Still, I would not accept that there was a problem that humans could not solve. I know that humans are damaging the planet. I understand how philosophical concepts—often taught as religion—say that God or someone out there approved of the 'rape-rip-and-run' approach to utilizing Earth's resources and other humans and other life forms. All of these things considered, I had a deep feeling that man could and would change course and define our future.

"I had never considered another player, a new god, if you will, a man-created super intelligence (SI) that is already present and day-by-day is amassing more data than our human minds together can process. Everything I had concluded I now questioned. How would our species survive if aggregated knowledge determined our future, instead of whim and caprice, or irrational human thought based on limited experience and knowledge? I started questioning things like data emphasis and standardized tests as if the students were programmable computers. I learned more about our existing education systems based on competition rather than cooperation. In fact, I wanted to study and understand educators who pointed out that the way we were following Industrial Revolution thinking and Industrial Age organization of human beings was only designed to make us complacent and easily enslaved as labor. I knew our schools had not worked for years. I came to the conclusion that man was in fact near extinction. But I still believe that we can rise above what is broken and come up with a way of partnering with SI to evolve humanity so that humans will have a brilliant future.

"I'm still working on that. That is where my energy is going now. In my high school, I can only identify a few students who would be curious enough to do a campfire. I might try and organize a campfire group so I can share the process with others.

"My remaining question is whether there will be enough of us to actually change the system."

Roberto: "I have learned that seeking help from state or federal government is difficult. I grew up knowing that the American Dream is not for everyone. I grew up watching the Feds confiscate the property and assets of people who had lived in the USA for decades, even some who served in the military, but were not born here. None were ever compensated for their homes, vehicles, businesses, stolen bank accounts or possessions. They were exploited.

"Most of the people of our heritage, like my grandparents, were brought here by mining companies who used them, paid them poorly, and then abandoned them when they were no longer needed or when the economy turned sour. They got the government to deport them back to Mexico or Central America. My family was lucky. My grandparents were exiled, but my parents, my sisters, brothers and I were born here. We're citizens, but have to be constantly on guard to not get picked up and harassed by ICE.

"I'm sharing this information because I have a completely different background than most of you. For people like me who have brown skin, the American history I have experienced is not the history you are taught. My daily life at school was often filled with fear, prejudice, or dealing with hostile and ignorant people.

"When I learned that there was a virtual class where I could meld in and participate without admission questions that were designed to put me in a box, I signed on. I love to learn and think. I'm curious. I want to contribute. I will go to a university. At first, like George, I could create an avatar to hide in. That is when my whole world changed and I was free of the society that bound me.

"I had to learn to trust to break free. I kept my avatar until I was certain no one would judge me by my externals. It was the first time I had the opportunity to work with others and focus on getting information and solving problems. In a very short time, I was contacting educators and authors and people who were sharing information. Research was a door that opened the world to me. I was on a team. We wanted to know about the qualities that made us human, and we wanted to compare that information with whatever it was that made machines intelligent.

"In just weeks my life changed for the better. I never imagined joining a virtual campfire on the Internet would have such a profound effect on me. It was like being held in a locked closet and then suddenly being released into the light. I think that is one of the promises of SI. I know it can be misused, but think of the human energy that can be released by focusing on learning how to get and use unlimited information that is available and then using it to make a contribution. I'm still reeling from information that really hit home.

"I have a lot of research to do about ACE—Adverse Childhood Experiences. If I ever become a parent or become a teacher, I will have kids in my classes that suffer from this abuse. They are in such pain that they cannot learn. As schools and families continue to fail something must be done.

"What major questions remain? I worry that SI will fall into the hands of those who will use it to destroy our species. What I have learned is that it can also be used to unleash the human qualities that create a better world."

Ron: "Most American high school graduates don't know that a university education is free in some countries in Europe if you have the portfolio. Many of our most talented students are recruited by Europeans and there is a real brain-drain from America. The kids whose parents are wealthy or have some connection to American universities—for example, legacy kids—and the privileged class who would never consider lowering themselves by using the public schools, send their kids where they can meet and rub shoulders with other privileged kids who then support each other through life. A good bad example is Brett Kavanaugh who has been placed on the Supreme Court—not out of merit it seems, but in spite of it.

"I mention this American reality because what we learned at the campfires is that given a level playing field and the opportunity to make a contribution, most human beings, regardless of gender, race, economics, or privilege can contribute to the advancement of humanity. The problem is that the systems in place do not free students to contribute. That is what our campfire team has been trying to identify and change.

"There are adjustments to the present education approaches that can overcome impediments that were put in place for other people and other times. What I call the 'educational reality' is that many of these social class, gender, race and wealth conditions have sorted our populations in such a way that a majority of students are limited in what they can accomplish and contribute to themselves and society. We will lose the contributions of many of our brightest, most creative citizens. We don't know who will have the 'original' answer to one of humanity's imminent threats. We need everyone's unique perspective to help.

"What major question remains? I think I've identified some; and our group of imperative seekers has identified a lot more. We focus on the predator lion in the bush, but the question is whether we can awaken our consciousness in time to realize it is the lioness that hunts us."

Claire: "I never lost contact with the friends I made around the first campfires. It's hard to believe I am so bonded to people I have never met face-to-face. I generally know where they live, but it doesn't matter. We worked together to find out some of the most important things about ourselves and all human beings.

"Thinking back over how this happened to me, I became empowered because I learned to work with others to address issues that affect my future and my life. Imagine that! I had been taught what to do and how to think. I was told to answer test questions with the answers I was given. I was taught that I had to perform as programmed or others would beat me to the prize, whatever that was. I did have a few teachers who wanted me to learn critical thinking skills, but the system was not designed to let me do that.

"In our first meetings, I was angry. I believed that a teacher's job is to tell us what to learn and how to regurgitate the information injected into our brains. I had to learn information deemed important by some control group who identified a common core of information and who devised ways to see that that core was taught. Those who thought that way designed punitive tests to ensure that it was taught. 'You will be assimilated into the Borg collective'. *Star Trek Next Generation* fans know what I mean.

"As a high school junior, I knew how to succeed in that system. I never questioned what was done to me. Then I met a mentor who said that I could learn as a member of a team, that others would join in and all of us, male, female, black, brown, privileged, or poor, whatever, would be equal and explore together. It took me by surprise. I wasn't even out of high school and I could accelerate my learning and grow without boundaries and limitations which were designed to keep me submissive. I asked myself, 'Self, what was all my schooling for?'

"In time I came to understand that all the skills I needed to take over my education, the foundation skills like reading, writing, basic arithmetic, and socialization were necessary if I wanted to learn how things worked and how to change them if they didn't work. I came to understand that if my reading skills were a hinderance I could accelerate my learning, get help if I needed it, and get to where I aspired to be. It was up to me, I had to be in charge of my education.

"It had been a long time since a teacher or parent sat down with me and went over a test that showed me what needed to be beefed up. But my teachers were forced to stop using tests to help identify student needs, because they had to teach for tests that were used to place, placate or punish those who did not do what some data-cruncher or fake reformer said must be done.

"Okay, enough of that. By the third campfire I knew that my personal problems with gender issues, vanity issues, and roles I had to play were no longer limitations. No one on our team knew or cared about my social position, preferences, or family background. All we cared about each other was solving challenges that impinged on our future and how my personal experiences could be drawn upon to contribute to the discussion and enrich perspectives. All energy was focused on research, gathering information and projecting our findings into our future.

"I want to add that learning to research or actually search for answers opened a whole new world to me. Because information is not owned or controlled anymore, I could explore other ways of thinking and get other insights into how things worked. My schooling had put blinders on me and tried to focus my development to serve a culture that no longer exists. Intuitively, I knew that. With SI, all human knowledge is available just for asking. I am learning how to ask.

"I am really troubled by what I have learned, especially about teaching, education, and the future of America. I didn't find the sources I needed for this information. I thought the teachers' unions—NEA and AFT—would be leading the fight to save our public schools. Then I learned that a majority of certified and experienced teachers have been driven out of the profession in a matter of years. Most parents have no idea what that means. They just want us kids safe and off the streets. I have a lot of research I want to do and perhaps I can light my own campfire.

"What major question remains? Can we really make an impact on the evolution of our educational systems in ways that prepare students for their future? The campfires have given us good places to start."

Dave: "I have had amazing educational experiences. In my university I was able to separate from the planned programming courses. Through the Honors College I began to get a global perspective. After leaving 'formal' education, I was free to travel and experience other cultures; to rub shoulders with people who seem to be different but are not.

"I learned that the basic nature of man has not changed in tens of thousands of years. I spent three years in Africa living with other humans who our American culture dismissively portrays as primitive. I learned we have much more in common than not. There is a strong sense of community there and many cultural groups are often in even greater touch with their own humanity.

"I keep up with advancements in artificial intelligence. There are benefits to enhanced data-gathering, analysis, and management tools. Access and utilization of these tools at the community level is pretty tough. Once gathered though, the data can be used to document abuses and advocate for protections that protect people's rights. As our world is increasingly tied together through technology, there are opportunities to shine a light on violations and bring the pressure of the international community to bear. I have seen the horror of what people are capable of. That is why I needed to balance my pessimism with hope, as I connected with other change agents around the campfires.

"I know the future is forming and that our cultures are not adapting well. But I keep a deep-seated belief that human nature can evolve. Around campfires with others who collaborate without the limitations of societal labels and conditioning, we are working to find information about how to preserve the spiritual side of humanity in beings that can inherit the universe. I think, as human beings evolve, they will be as different from us as we are from apes. Maybe through our partnership with SI we will physically and spiritually transcend into a very different state of being. I wonder. Will we be prepared for non-organic entities taking over for us biological entities if that is the answer?

"What major question remains? Can we separate the animal and reptilian parts of humans from the spiritual parts?"

Ken: "I'm Native American. That means I have

to check a separate box on census forms, job applications, education applications, and even medical forms. I think the majority of non-indigenous people think I'm different, maybe even savage-human. For the first time in my life, I got into a program that wasn't interested in my heritage, race, gender, sexual preference, family wealth, or any of the ways society uses to sort people. To participate, all I had to do was show up and work with others to find information and answers to pressing problems.

"The campfires are the first time in my life that I was equal and accepted. If I could live in a virtual world, free of labels and bigotry, I would—well, in fact, that is what I do when I work collaboratively with others to solve problems.

"I was ashamed to be Native American. The BIE schools were run to make us white. Yes, even in the mid-2000s when I was in elementary school, it was beaten into me that what my ancestors valued was wrong and would keep us from becoming civilized.

"Then, I got to go to public school. Most of the teachers were nice people, but they were afraid to let us out unsupervised during recess because in the wild of our playground we were a strong presence with a lot of energy. We played hard. We had been forced to sit and not move for hours while we were talked at or given worksheets. The best days were when they brought in elders from Native American tribes who lived in the area. It didn't happen very often. The teachers let us know that they felt sorry for these old people because they didn't bathe and often didn't eat. Obviously, these people were inferior, just look at them.

"I listened to the elders. I heard stories about my people. Stories I had never heard. Stories that were filled with pride, respect, and purpose. I wish I had listened more and discounted them less. But they sparked something in me and I taught myself to read and checked books out from the school library. I spent time on the 'rez' and listened. I did better in school, but I had a divided heart.

"I lived two lives. My parents knew, but they were broken by the Indian schools and were afraid for me. I convinced them that I was okay, and that my time reading Native American stuff and researching all sorts of things that interested me didn't put us in danger.

"I liked the safety and expansiveness of virtual places. I joined Doc's campfires because I was curious and didn't have to identify myself. Now, I'm not alone anymore and I have grown proud of my heritage.

"What major question remains—like what am I still looking for? Wisdom about how we will be respectful of all other species on our planet. How we can live our lives with reciprocity and balance. I want to be more aware of connections rather than differences, like the Blackfoot idea of evolving spirit."

Dan: "I know the importance of our work and I am doing this because I was lucky enough to have the opportunity. I grew up in an Asian neighborhood in San Francisco. Before this, I never had opportunities to make a contribution, nor did anyone I know. We were always told that once we grew up, then we could participate. I look forward to hanging out with my friends; to collaborate with them as we gather around our own virtual campfires and search for solutions to the challenges we face in our lives every day.

"If we change our education system to one that encourages cooperation and problem-solving, something we all learned from the research we did via these campfire meetings, we will create teams of people of all ages who already know how to work together to research and solve real problems. We will be stronger and less governed by fear and competition. I look forward to working in that kind of world.

"What is the one thing that I am really concerned about? Super intelligence and data compilation that will be used to amplify our most predatory and short sighted/self-serving and destructive tendencies."

Mary: "My ancestors, my family, have been in

this part of the USA since before the Revolutionary War. We are descendants of those who came from Europe (Spain) and settled in this area which is now called New Mexico. Then, this land was part of Mexico, but our family traditions are European. That is good and bad. The bad part is that our lands and population were coveted by others who ignored our rights and took our lands. This was common practice in the conquest of the West. We were treated almost as badly as the Native Americans. As a subject people who had no rights, we suffered at the whims of evil people who imposed their will on us. They ignored what we were and had accomplished. In time, they Americanized us.

"That exploitation fostered a hatred of Mexicans as an excuse for taking their land, killing their people, and ignoring human rights. I grew up a victim of this hatred and bigotry. In my schools there was always a color wall that kept us separate. People of my heritage were not included and could not contribute. I was often called a beaner. I could slide through by pretending that I had no feelings and agreed with the majority. My bitterness turned to self-damage. Burning and cutting seemed to take the emotional pain away.

"In my heart, I wanted to be accepted as me; to be loved not rejected by those around me. Then one day, I learned about the campfires and the fact that I could participate regardless of heritage, religion, gender, or previous acts against the system. I joined because I could be me and participate without other labels being used to stymie me. Within weeks I was another person, valued for my contributions. I had a lot of catching up to do to be able to read and process information, but I had strong motivation to do this and I kept up with other members of our team. When I was certain that restrictions were gone, I grew quickly and worked hard to heal my damaged self. Now I know how to take over my own education and who knows what I can contribute? Speaking of contributing, I just found this article by Ben Dickson in *Tech Talks*. May 3, 2021: "4 Key Misunderstandings in AI," from *Demystifying AI*.

"The article really made me think about how fast our understanding and information about machine intelligence is evolving. As I read Dickson's views, I realized that they were several years behind and presented information that is already out of date. Our research indicates that SI is gaining information at an amazing rate and already surpasses many of the limitations listed in the article. The campfires are over, but I keep finding new sources of information.

"What is the major unsolved issue? How do we convince educators to build collaborative, not competitive systems? How do we learn to deal with societies that create damaged children, like I was damaged and worse, who do not get the support needed in the public schools?

"I never believed that a system as petrified as our education system could be changed. Now, I really think it can."

Frank: "I suffered the chaos and evil created by politicians and greed. Louisiana, and especially New Orleans schools, were heavily damaged by hurricane Katrina on August 29, 2005. After Katrina I went to what they call charter schools which were really partial schools led by those who wanted access to tax dollars, not programs for kids. If I learned anything, it was that I was a commodity that could be bought or sold depending on who could profit. This gave the pickers an opportunity to exploit children. If my parents had not worked with me to master the basics, I, like most of my friends, would have been deprived of the functioning skills necessary to raise above ignorance and poverty. I worry the private corporations controlling charter schools for their own profit have largely succeeded in creating a lost generation as a result.

"No university would consider accepting me as my SAT and ACT scores reflected that I had not been fed the selected data necessary to test well. My parents were trapped in the area because they had lost everything in the hurricane. All my mom and dad could do was help me take charge of my own learning and utilize community resources like the public library. I had to leave my house in order to get on line. I found most of what I knew on virtual sites. Finally, the librarian took pity on me and invited me into her world of books and information. She was overwhelmed with student requests for help and had no budget to provide many of the services needed.

"Everything seemed stacked against me. I had to work twice as hard for everything. I was poor, had a deep southern accent, barely knew my basics, was considered white trash by the politicians in power, and had no one in the education system to turn to. One day, I learned about a class—no, a campfire meeting where I could participate with no questions asked. The rest is what you know of me—Frank a fellow contributor, researcher and problem-solver. But for this opportunity, I could not progress to help my family. Oh, and SI may be the tool we need.

"What is the major unsolved issue? Will human beings evolve so that we can positively focus human energy instead of thwarting it?"

Doc: "Thank you all for your insights. I too have learned a great deal during our time together. During these sessions, we have sought answers to questions about our future, our place in it, and we've explored some of the deep structural changes needed to make our education system relevant in a rapidly changing world dominated by technology. As we worked together, we found it really didn't matter if we lived on separate continents or sat at computers in a physical classroom. What matters is that we did not judge others by race, gender, position in society, or any limiting ways of discounting one another's contributions. We worked collaboratively and our team of learners and problem solvers was stronger as a result.

"As we identified problems in our education system and gained a better understanding of machine intelligence, we modeled a different learning approach that used our devices to access vast amounts of information. Our style of learning focused on collaboration and contribution. Through shared information and our ongoing dialog around ideas, we identified competencies necessary for the survival of our species and our democracy. We are better prepared to embrace the positive aspects of SI as a partner and guard against its' abuse.

"We have also reached out and found other people who are searching for solutions. As we go forward, separately or around other campfires, we will all continue to connect with sources of information and ideas that will lead us to new possibilities. Thanks again for your contributions and your commitment to the process. This is the dawn of your new age."

Chapter 10

Epilogue

What is a student? The property of the state? A vessel to be filled only with the needs and desires of those in control? Or, are teachers empowered to individualize the learning path of each individual student and work collaboratively with that student as they become a fully realized human being with the self-regulated power to make a unique contribution to the human race.

What is a school? A warehouse to keep kids safe while the parents serve their masters? A place to regulate and control thought? A social place where students are taught to conform to society's standards? Or, is it a collaborative experience that is not necessarily tied to a physical space; an experience that rewards cooperative investigative behavior focused on open-ended solutions to real-world problems. The school must become a place where involvement, creativity, respectful dialog, and differences are integrated into the over-arching learning philosophy.

Educator Jalynn Bacon-Dorow has pointed out, "As educators, we encourage students to set the world on fire with their ideas, knowledge, critical analyses, and creativity. We want them to become life-long learners, contributors to society, and a positive human presence in a technology-driven world."

From the onset, *Human Competence: Imperatives* set out to expose the inequities inherent in today's standardized educational systems and to offer an alternative approach. This approach focused on the skills and competencies *all* students need *now* to flourish in a balanced partnership with AI/SI; to ensure the survival of our species.

Around a series of campfires, a diverse cohort of young adults courageously explored the exploding superpowers of artificial intelligence and how to harness this super intelligence for the betterment of all humankind. They took this challenge on with a heightened sense of urgency, realizing the clock is ticking and that the needed educational shifts will be met with strong resistance by those who benefit most from the status quo.

They concluded the current "one size fits all" instructional model is inherently ineffective and that a new paradigm will be required. The new approach will need to be rooted in curiosity and wonder, and honor variability. They realized the campfire experience of collaboration and problem solving was a model for the needed shift. A connection was made to the campfire's norms of mutual respect, collaboration, inter-dependence, acceptance, safety, belonging, voice, and choice in the shelter of authenticity and risk-taking without judgment. In the end, they understood that diversity is a strength, as is a focus on problem-solving. These are the conditions that will prepare our children for their technology-rich future and not our industrial past. *It's the system that is broken, not our kids!*

The programmatic drivers of a new school system should include intellectual rigor, activism, equity, connection, clarity, and personal/community well-being. We must evolve and adapt if our species is to survive . . . it is an existential imperative!

> "It is not the strongest of the species that survives, nor the most intelligent; it is the one most adaptable to change."
>
> —Charles Darwin

If there is to be change, we need to build campfires and share information as we transform ourselves and incorporate the benefits of the amazing world of information that is now available. Or we can teach students to sit quietly, keep their books open, and their mouths shut.

Those connected with this approach to education urge you all to: Start your campfires. Stir the embers. Prepare for what is coming in your time. Remember, hope burns brightest in those who believe in their ability to impact the future.

Annotated References

Recommended readings and online documentaries that provide more detailed context for concepts touched upon in this work:

The History Of AI. A documentary on YouTube that delves deeper into AI, It is dated but very informative. (https://www.youtube.com/watch?v=R3YFx-F0n8n8.)

Sapiens: A Brief History of Humankind, by Yuval Noah Harari. Harper Collins. 2015. Other important reads by Harari: *Homo Deus, A Brief history of Tomorrow*, and *21 Lessons for the 21st Century*. YouTube has put up many interviews and discussions with Harari. Most of these are vital to our understanding of many issues touched upon in *Human Competence: Imperatives*. Self-directed learners will take the time, in the future, to understand this great historian and philosopher's insights.

Life 3.0: Being Human In The Age Of Artificial Intelligence, by Max Tegmark. Vintage Books. 2018. Once you read the Preface—you will delve into the book and find answers to many of your questions about our future.

The Right Drivers For Whole System Success, by Michael Fullan. A position paper produced in Australia by Centre for Strategic Education. Michael Fullan is perhaps the most effective leader for educational change today. His many books and design projects have helped educators around the world advance education for the future.

Learner Centered Innovation: Spark Curiosity, Ignite Passion and Unleash Genius, by Dr. Katie Martin. 2018. Impress, LP (her works are available at Amazon.) She is VP of Leadership and Learning at Altitude Learning. She teaches at the graduate school of education at High Tech High and is on the board of Real World Scholars. She is involved at the university, district and school level.

Balance With Blended Learning, also *Blended Learning In Action*, and *Power Up With Blended Learning*, by Dr. Catlin R. Tucker. Corwin Press. 2020. Katie Novak and Catlin Tucker, *UDL and Blended Learning*.

2021. We are awed by the work of these great educators.

Empower, by John Spencer and AJ Juliani, 2017. Amazon. We discovered Spencer and were delighted to share his insights.

Hackers Used To Be Humans. Soon AIs Will Hack Humanity by Bruce Schneier. WIRED. 04.19.202. A great article that supports SI.

The Death and Life of the Great American School System, and *Slaying Goliath: The Passionate Resistance to Privatization*, and *Reign of Error: The Hoax of the Privatization Movement* and the *Danger to America's Public Education*, by Dr. Diane Ravitch. These are pivotal works in American education today. Diane Ravitch's blogs are the #1 way to keep up with current issues in education.

Definitions

Artificial—False. Fake. Mock. Non-natural, not human made, not occurring naturally, synthetic, not natural or real.

Intelligence—The ability to acquire knowledge and skills. Powers of reasoning judgement reason, the ability to learn and understand or to deal with new or trying situations. The capacity for logic, understanding, self-awareness, learning, emotional knowledge, planning, creativity, critical thinking.

Machine Intelligence—Artificial intelligence (AI) is intelligence demonstrated by machines, unlike the natural intelligence displayed by humans and animals that involves consciousness and emotionality.

Machine—An apparatus using or applying mechanical powers.

Augmented Artificial Intelligence—In this context, a way to use artificial intelligence to expand learning opportunities in education. Augmentation is currently utilized to varying degrees by educators.

Super Intelligence (SI)—Within the world of AI, there are several levels of sophistication and development. Augmented AI is already a basic part of our daily activities. As we now apply it, it is a tool to enhance education and almost every human activity. It can be extremely useful, but it is not what is driving the future.

What we have learned is that the 'genius' level of AI is a Super Intelligence (SI). As these artificial intelligence algorithms become more complex, they are gaining the ability to mimic how the human brain works and surpass it in many functional areas. SI is becoming an advanced intelligence in its own right. As SI evolves, it has the potential to become a sentient entity; a new life form on our planet. This will create all kinds of ethical and moral debates about who controls SI.

Acknowledgements

The I is We. I would especially like to thank Dan Kenley, my co-conspirator and an active contributor to this book. Over the years, Dan has accomplished so much as an educator. He is a dear friend and collaborator. He challenges us every day to imagine schools that inspire students.

Dr. Norman K. Eck, an educator and leader, has provided advice and critiques that are value-added.

Thank you to my editor, Jalynn Bacon-Dorow who excels in creativity and critical thinking.

Special thanks to my family. My wife Jo and our sons, Alex and David, have provided ongoing support throughout the development of this book. Jo's help on all my books has been invaluable.

About the Author

Ed Berger began teaching high school in the Cherry Creek District near Denver, Colorado in 1961. During his public school career he pioneered many interdisciplinary, supplemental, enrichment programs that stressed experiential 'hands-on' education.

In 1968, he began building his dream school and research center near Cortez in Southwest Colorado. In 1969-70 Ed spent a year studying education programs in twenty-two nations around the world. When he returned to the U.S. he continued building his dream. After 6 years, the school and research center found its final home on 80 acres of wild land west of Cortez on Crow Canyon where it still continues to serve students of all ages today.

Ed earned his doctorate in education in 1975. He is an education advocate and consultant. He lives with his wife Jo, in Prescott, Arizona.

www.ingramcontent.com/pod-product-compliance
Lightning Source LLC
LaVergne TN
LVHW012052160826
845678LV00014B/2801